OLD TIME COLORADO COWBOY

REFLECTIONS

Written by: Henry F. Deter
Narrated by: Susan Eldringhoff

First published by AuthorHouse 03/21/05

ISBN: 1-4208-3572-6 (sc)

Printed in the United States of America
Bloomington, Indiana

This book is printed on acid-free paper.

authorHOUSE

1663 LIBERTY DRIVE, SUITE 200
BLOOMINGTON, INDIANA 47403
(800) 839-8640
www.authorhouse.com

CONTENTS

CONTENTS (Continued)

"OLD TIME COLORADO COWBOY REFLECTIONS"

BY HENRY F. DETER
Narration by Susan Eldringhoff

Introduction

This book is a collection of stories written by my Grandfather, Henry Francis Deter, throughout his lifetime. They are not "Wild West" stories like we've all seen in the movies, they are real west stories about his life, and his reflections of life as an old time Cowboy. The stories were all hand written in pencil, on a variety of paper, from tablets to index cards, all very neat and legible. It also includes a few newspaper clippings, and other items, found amongst his papers, which he had saved, in some cases, for fifty or sixty years.

He was born in Deer Trail, Colorado in 1894, and passed away there in 1986 at the age of 91. Our family considers ourselves so fortunate to have had a Grandfather who recorded, in these stories, so much of his life and the history of the area. He loved history, the old west, the Deer Trail area where he lived all his life, his family, and the United States of America.

Although these stories, in his words, mean more to our family than they possibly could to anyone else, they also contain so much old west, real west history that we wanted to share them. So much of the everyday life described in these stories is typical of all families who came west in the pioneering and homesteading days. The stories have been printed here just as they were written. They were not necessarily written in the order which they appear in this book, very few had dates, so we don't know the order or time frame of when they were written. Separate narrative is added, (*in italics*), when needed in order to set up the people, places, and events in the stories, and footnotes with additional information, when known.

Henry attended the one room "Deter Price School" to the eighth grade. High School was not available nor an option in that era of the west. He went on his first roundup at the age of 14 and a few years later left home to work on other ranches. He served in France in World War I. Grover Cleveland was President when he was born, and oh the changes he saw in his lifetime. He was practically born on a horse, grew up when a horse was a man's only form of transportation, then watched a man walk on the moon from his TV set in his own living room.

Henry's father, Philip Deter, was born in 1865, the year President Abraham Lincoln was assassinated. He left his home in LaGrange, Indiana at the age of 16, and headed for Texas. With the Civil War still being fresh on the minds of the Southerners, being from Indiana, he was called a "Yankee", and didn't receive a real warm reception. So he took a job as a drover with a trail herd, and came to Colorado, and to Deer Trail in 1882, and stayed. He worked as a cowboy for ranches in the area and on many roundups. He eventually became a roundup cook, because a cook got $90 a month compared to a cowpuncher's $30 a month. He ranched on the open range at Deer Trail, eventually homesteading and finally acquiring a 10,000 plus acre ranch. He rode his 33 year-old horse in the Deer Trail Rodeo Parade a few days prior to his 100th birthday. He passed away in 1966 at the age of 101.

He said when he first came to Deer Trail there were a few unfriendly Indians about 30 miles away, but he just steered clear of them, and there was a large buffalo herd that grazed just east of Deer Trail. Phil knew Pat Garrett, who shot Billy the Kid, and Phil bought the Kid's blue roan horse after the Kid was shot in Texas. He saw Buffalo Bill a few times, but said he wasn't good enough to ride in his Wild West Show.

Henry Deter helped organize a birthday celebration for his sister Maria in 1941, which became the 'Old Timers Roundup', and has been held annually since that time. In about 1950, Henry asked his Dad, Phil Sr., who was then 85, to reminisce about the early history of Deer Trail, for the Old Timers Roundup.

PHIL DETER, Sr. reminiscing for the "Old Timers"

A few notes of the early history of Deer Trail, as I recall are:
The first person to be buried in the Deer Trail Cemetery[1] was a man by the name of "White"[2]. He was killed when he was bucked off a horse. He worked for a man named "Tom Shreves", who had the old seven diamond inverted seven brand, and had a camp on the Muddy, close to where the Noonen reservoir is now.

---

[1] Evergreen Cemetery in Deer Trail, establishment date unknown, it was already in existence in 1870 when the railroad came through. No records were kept in those early days, and what records were later kept were destroyed in the 1965 flood in Deer Trail. There is a vast section of the Cemetery with old unmarked graves. Some were never marked, some of their crude markers just didn't stand the test of time.

[2] One of the many early graves, now without a marker, and no one left who knows where it is located.

4

One of the next graves that is up there, is the one with the rock slabs piled around it. It is the grave of the wife of Nels Nelson.[3] She died at the old "Three Ring" ranch[4] and her body was hauled there in a lumber wagon. Around one hundred cowboys rode to the funeral on horseback, some coming from as far away as Greeley and Rocky Ford.

The last trail herd that was branded in Deer Trail, was late in the fall in 1884. They were 1400 head of little southern yearlings, very thin and poor. They were owned by C. B. Rhodes, and cost $9.00 per head. There was a big branding chute at the Deer Trail Stockyards, and the yards were much larger than they are now. The winter of 1884 was a hard winter. Cattle died all over the country, and there was no feed. All but six of the 1400 head of cattle died. This broke Rhodes, but he got another start and became rich.

It was a great fad in the early days in Deer Trail, that if a newcomer came to town, a "tenderfoot", as they called them in those days, to make him "dance". So one day an old rancher, by the name of Ritson, had a few drinks, and saw a young fellow standing over on the depot platform. He said, "I guess I'll go over and make that tenderfoot dance". He went over and said "Young man can you dance?" The young man said he could, so Ritson told him to get at it, and shot a couple times at his feet. The "tenderfoot" shuffled around a few times until he got a good chance, and he hit the rancher in the jaw. It took three hours to bring the old man to, and that ended making the "tenderfoot" dance.

---

[3] Polly Nelson 1860-1885.
[4] Located on East Bijou, between Deer Trail and Agate, Colorado.

HENRY F. DETER

I was born November 20, 1894, in a sod house, about 4 miles northwest of Deer Trail, where my parents had homesteaded in the 1880s. I grew up there about like every kid raised on a ranch. The hazards of wondering away, of falling in a water hole, and of being bitten by a rattlesnake, were always on my mother's mind. Several rattlers were killed close to the sod house.

This story was related to me by my Mother, and was probably my first experience with a cow. My Dad went to Las Vegas, New Mexico and purchased two carloads of longhorn heifers in 1897 and shipped them to Deer Trail.[1] Hay was short in those times so the heifers had to exist on dry grass through the winters. One of them got thin and weak. My Dad hauled her in on a sled and put her in the hay corral by a small stack of hay. I wandered out of my mothers sight one day and crawled in the hay corral where the heifer was. I walked up to her and slapped her and about scared her out of her hide. She could not get up, so every time I slapped her she would bawl. My Mother heard her and that was how she found me.

For most of the early years, cattle and horses were the only animals on the ranch. We milked one cow. Cattle and horses was the only conversation I ever heard. When I grew up and learned to ride, to be a cowboy was my ambition. After a few years, I learned how to handle cattle and all kinds of horses. I went everywhere on a horse and rode many miles in those days.

I worked on ranches in different parts of Colorado, in North Park for Andrew Norrel, in Gunnison for Scobey and others, in Montana for the Howard Bros., 35 miles south of Forsyth. I repped[2] for them on the roundup with the Dutchman "S" outfit. I rode with or visited several roundup wagons in this country, the Hank Nordloh, the D lazy T Cattle Co., the Hashknife, the Sherrer Ranch. The Moore wagon[3] was the one I worked with for several years, the Sanford wagon I was with on the last roundup, about 1915.

I had the thrill and pleasure of riding many famous bucking horses some on ranches and at Rodeos. I rode at Cheyenne Frontier Days, in the finals for the "Champion Bronco Buster", at Gunnison, Colo. Cattleman's Days, at Hugo, at Limon, at Byers, at Matheson, at Fort Morgan, at Brush, at Greeley, at Kiowa, and at the Joe Connell Ranch Rodeo, the Carey Ranch Rodeo, and here at Deer Trail. Then on the roundup I would ride outlaws[4] brought from some ranches.

---

[1] by rail

[2] "represented" a ranch or brand on a roundup. This meant you were responsible for counting, branding, or sorting off all the cattle for that ranch or brand.

[3] each roundup was known by the name of the roundup boss, sometimes a ranch owner, who furnished the chuckwagon to feed the cowboys, (usually the larger ranches). (more about roundups in following stories)

[4] bucking horses that were considered too wild and mean to be broken to ride.

My father Philip Deter came here in 1882 from Indiana. My mother Julia O'Connor Deter came here from New York state. My wife Helen Compton Deter was born in Nebraska, we were married in 1926. We are the parents of three children. Joann Deter LeValley lives at Hotchkiss, Colo. She has been a teacher there for many years. Andree Deter Van Matre lives at Deer Trail and owns a small motel, liquor store, and gasoline filling station complex. Brian Deter lives at Greeley and he and his wife are brand inspectors.

> I've met a heap o' cowboys and some was real top hands,
> I've seen a million cattle, and read a lot o' brands,
> I've seen some hard old winters, when nearly all the cattle died.
> I've rode some cuttin' horses that could turn right out of their hides.
> I've ate my share o' beefsteak, and drank some whiskey, too,
> An' did a little dancin' with nothin' else to do.
> Been bucked off old outlaws that I couldn't start to ride,
> An' saw some fine old buddies go over the Great Divide.
> With friends and family now, I'm makin' my last stand.
> An' hopin' to be horseback when I reach the Promised Land.[5]

I am retired now having sold my ranch two years ago. Here are some of the history of my days on the small ranch I owned. I lived there 45 years, which equals 16,425 days, which equals 394,200 hours. I estimated I worked one half of the time, which equaled 197,100 hours, about $4.00 per hour equaled the price of the land.

---

[5] Henry did not write this poem, (author unknown), but he evidently thought it appropriate to describe his life.

DEER TRAIL. COLORADO

If you had traveled across the empty plains of eastern Colorado Territory to the town of Deer Trail, you would have seen a true western frontier town in the best tradition of the old west. Deer Trail, a name which will live in the annals of history.

Picture old time saloons jammed with suntanned cowboys, with 45s in their belts, just off the long trail from Texas with herds of longhorn cattle. Then picture the open unfenced country, the unpaved streets and gambling games and casual gunplay. Many colorful characters have passed through or lived in the Deer Trail area, including gunslingers, famous cowboys and cattlemen.

Ages before Deer Trail, the area was covered with water from 300 to 1600 feet deep. The lake reaching from about Muddy creek on the east to as far as Boulder, Colo. on the west. Thousands of years ago the wind from the north and west blew it full of sand, making a desert of the country for several hundred years. Then nature covered the desert with many varieties of good grass, creating a vast grazing area. Then came great herds of buffalo roaming over the undulating grassland. They were hunted for food and for their skins by the Indians.

About 1920 the town of Deer Trail decided to explore deeper for a well for city water, and discovered that the sands, known as the "Fox Hills", were saturated with an abundance of pure soft water and had enough pressure to flow 18 feet above ground at that time. Today almost every ranch and farm in the surrounding area has one or more of these wells.

Then came the white man, most of them were cattlemen and cowboys with an idea of replacing the buffalo with cattle. Then a few cattlemen entered the country with their herds of longhorn cattle. Chief among the owners was John Hittson, whose brand was on thousands of cattle. In a few years many large sheep ranchers moved in on the open range of the same area.

Then came the prairie schooner and the stagecoach crossing the great plains, bringing new people. All were headed for the newly discovered gold fields in the mountains. The accounts and reports of their travels opened the way for the pioneer ranchers and farmers who settled in the lush valleys along the trail.

Traffic to the west came over one trail that came through and had a camp where Deer Trail is today. History tells us a great deal of the hardships and privations and the Indian trouble, and how camps and forts were established for the protection of these immigrants.

Then came the Railroad, in 1869, platting and surveying the Deer Trail town site on November 11, 1875.

Many of the large cattle and horse ranches had been located close to Deer Trail before the railway came through. One of the largest shipping points was Deer Trail. Many train loads of cattle were loaded and shipped from Deer Trail east to the markets for beef and hides. Also many loads of sheep and wool were shipped from Deer Trail.

Then came the big problems and hardships when it was discovered that sometimes it was dry here, that droughts and hard winters and big blizzards came every few years. The droughts caused overgrazing and the hard winters caused huge losses of cattle and sheep. Historians wrote about how the combination of drought and a hard winter caused the loss of great herds of cattle and sheep in 1878. But the winter of 1885-86 is claimed by every historian as being the worst ever known. Thousands of cattle and sheep perished. Pioneer August Beuck of Agate told of seeing so many carcasses floating in the Arkansas River that it would have been possible to walk across stepping on the dead cattle.

These severe snowstorms have continued through history. In October 1902 one took the toll of thousands of cattle, sheep, and horses. Another storm occurred in March, 1910, which was considered one of the worst ever, and although it lasted only 24 hours, it killed hundreds of cattle and sheep. Three feet of snow fell in 1913-14, and three and a half feet of snow fell in 1946. Many more such storms have occurred through the years, but the early blizzard and long hard winter of 1972-73 will be talked about for many years to come, as the most severe in modern times.

When a wagon train rolled into Deer Trail and somebody yelled "ride 'em cowboy" it was July 4, 1869[1], and the main event was the Bronco Busting Contest being held for the first time anywhere. Crowning the champion bronco buster of the plains that day. Riding and roping have had a big part in the heritage of Deer Trail. The professionals that came here met their match with the bucking horses and cowboys that were here.

Many rodeos have been held in Deer Trail since 1869, and are still being held annually, sponsored by the Deer Trail Jockey Club, an organization with membership numbering in three figures, featuring one of the best amateur contests in Colorado.

The rules and equipment have changed many times in 100 years. There were no chutes for saddling the horses. The horses were eared down[2] and turned loose in the open. The bareback riders had nothing but a mane hold[3], and the saddle bronc riders with a straight forked saddle[4]. Sometimes they used a Levi jacket for a "saddle roll"[5], in later years it was outlawed.

---

[1] Deer Trail is recorded as the "Home of the World's First Rodeo", by the Colorado State Legislature, Rodeo Hall of Fame, and the Guinness Book of World Records.

[2] A cowboy would grab around a horse's neck or head and bite down hard on his ear. This evidently distracted the horse enough to make him settle down a little so he could be mounted or saddled.

[3] nothing to hold on to but the horses mane.

[4] a saddle with no swells. Swells are a raised portion at the front of the saddle on both sides of the saddle horn.

[5] a jacket rolled up and put in front of both upper thighs of the rider, to take the place of swells on a saddle.

If you have viewed the panorama of the Rockies from the high ridges surrounding Deer Trail, you have seen them appear as giant icebergs. Or at times they appear to be a light pinkish color, and other times they are the color of gold, and many times they appear as huge chunks of silver lying on the earth's surface. Or you have seen them as an uneven blue ridge on the western horizon just after sun down on some late fall days.

You can see lakes near Deer Trail where they are far from water, known as hot weather mirages. You can see cattle standing in water about knee deep, or you can see a river, about four or five feet deep, running across the prairie, always to the north west. You can see cattle walking close to these rivers. At times the lakes appear to stay in one place for hours, probably about a mile distant, but will disappear in a moment if approached. By looking north and west you can see the creeks, including the trees and any ranch buildings, raised above the hilltops by the optical illusion of cold weather mirages, when the temperature falls to 15 to 20 degrees below zero.

In the 1880s, Colorado was still a frontier and was the fabulous land of adventure and golden opportunity. It had been open to hardy men and still was. Many stayed and grew up with the ways of the "West", such were the pioneers that we have known, who became constructive and respected citizens.

Then came a big change in ranching. Meadows were fenced, hay was stacked in the summer to supplement the grass for winter feeding, to carry the cattle through the hard winters. The picturesque cowboy of the old west and the wide open range had gone in the timeless past as have the longhorn cattle and wild horse, which roamed freely from Canada to Mexico.

After the turn of the century, a few homesteaders came into the country. Happenings of the past were forgotten, the opportunities were advertised everywhere in the east. By about 1910, most of the government land was filed on. The great herds of longhorn cattle had vanished.

Sod houses and many other kinds of homestead shanties were the homes of the people who came from the eastern states. The descendents of some of this wave of settlers remain to this day. Deer Trail was the headquarters for the U.S. Land Commissioner for this area, the office was located in the old Hotel. Many of these homesteaders proved their right to title to the homestead and through this office received the patent to their land without leaving Deer Trail. "Proving up" was the term they used[6], and the document called the patent at that time, is known as the deed.

We have heard of wagon trains and all of the belongings that people took with them on these long journeys across the plains. The "immigrant trains" were also loaded with even more belongings. At times several immigrant railroad cars came into Deer Trail. Some people brought four or five milk cows, a team of horses, a wagon and a buggy, chickens and pigs, all of the furniture they owned,

---

[6] Homesteaders were required to build on, and occupy their 160 acres for a period of 5 years, and plow 40 acres, (later changed to 320 acres, plowing 80). When this was accomplished, they were said to have proven up on the land and were granted ownership through a patent or deed.

plus plows and tools, and some brought fencing material, and their cats and dogs and other pets. It was quite a sight, sometimes amusing, watching them unload a car and get ready to move out on a bare hill where there was no water, no fence, and what looked like no grass to them, after coming from a tall grass country back east.

Local people were the shareholders and officers of the Deer Trail State Bank, which was granted a charter in 1910. This bank proved to be a great and useful asset to the town and community. The original bank building stands today across the street from the old hotel building.

During World War I, the Deer Trail Livestock Loan Association was organized, with their office in the bank. Also having the same men for officers as the bank, and using monies for loans that came through the bank. During the war and after, prices of cattle and sheep and all other things inflated two or three times. Good cows brought $120 to $140 per head, and good ewes from $15 to $25 per head. These organizations had done a brisk business in war time, especially with livestock loans. After the war, demand dropped off, prices sagged to a level 40 years back in time, old timers claimed. Cows at $25 per head and ewes at $1 to $2 per head. So the bank being faced with this disaster was forced to close its doors. The bank was refinanced later, but failed in a short time, never to reopen. At the time the Deer Trail State Bank was booming, another charter was granted to the First National Bank of Deer Trail. It also had financial reverses and was forced to close its doors, never to reopen.

Deer Trail was still a good town even after all of the disasters and declines. The Kansas Pacific Railroad Company laid out the site of the old town, and stockyards in 1875. It was designed to accommodate handling large herds of longhorn cattle. While shipping from here at that time, eleven cattle cars could be loaded at one time.

A few years ago the railroad donated the old depot building, built in 1881, to the Deer Trail Pioneer Historical Society to be used as a museum. It was moved to the north end of City Park, and is now a western historical museum. Not a very handsome or beautiful building, but unchanged. They have collected many authentic western articles, such as copper boilers, wash boards, shoe repair stands and lasts[7], churns, kraut cutters, lanterns, dresses and gowns, bits, spurs, old time saddles, and many other western things. Included is a "Bon I. Look" whiskey jug. Bon I. Look owned a general store in Denver. The stock contained nearly everything, including Bon I. Look Whiskey. Twice a year his wagon visited every ranch in the country selling supplies. In the spring, for summer needs, and in the fall for winter and school supplies, and always lots of Bon I. Look Whiskey.

---

[7] Lasts were metal shoe forms placed inside the shoe, then turned upside down and placed on a shoe stand, to provide a solid sturdy foundation to tack a new sole onto a boot or shoe. They came in many different sizes to fit each size shoe.

11

Following is a "portion" of a story, (pages 4 & 5). Unfortunately, we have not been able to find the beginning. It fits with the Deer Trail Story, as this portion talks about the old hotel in Deer Trail, located on First and Elm. The original Hotel, which sat near that location, owned by Gideon Burton, burned to the ground in 1910.

The history of the Kansas Pacific Railway Company through this State comprised the grant of all of the odd numbered sections of land, by the United States for the construction of a railway. Section 13 Township 5 Range 60, where the town of Deer Trail is, is one of the sections included in that grant, which extended twenty miles on each side of the railway.

A map laying out, platting and subdividing a portion of Section 13, Township 5, Range 60, dated November 11, 1875, was signed by Robert Carr, President and D. M. Edgerton, Secretary of the Kansas Pacific Railway Company. It designated the "Town of Deer Trail", granting perpetual right of way to the public over all streets and avenues on this map.

A deed dated September 14, 1876, conveyed Lot 1, Block 6, Town of Deer Trail, signed by Adolph Meier, trustee, of Kansas Pacific Railway Co., to Edward Russell. (This is where the Hotel sets at present.) These buildings and improvements comprised a store, warehouse, and a house. Some of the later owners were Finis P. Ernest, Burchard Dillon and Company, and George F. Hodge. The taxes on the property was fourteen dollars and seventy-five cents in the year 1877.

A warranty deed dated March 9, 1919 conveyed, Lot 1, Block 6, from Gideon L. Burton to Allen J. Cummins who built the existing Hotel.

The following two stories were written by Anne H. Casey from interviews she did with Henry Deter in the spring of 1977, when he was 83. She was evidently doing research on historical sites in Arapahoe County. A copy of what she had written was found with Grandpa's other stories. I am including only portions of it here, as some of the facts are repeated in other of his stories.

DEER TRAIL CEMETERY

No one knows who was first buried in the Evergreen Cemetery. The burial plot is located approximately a tenth of a mile east of Deer Trail on a hill. It can be reached by following Cedar Street under the I-70 underpass and up the hillside towards the prairie. Hank Deter surmises that early pioneers in the Deer Trail area were buried there.

The cemetery was surveyed and platted at the same time as the town on November 11, 1875. The oldest known grave is that of Leonard Stanley who was buried three months after the platting on February 28, 1876. Stanley died mysteriously. He and a partner were herding horses on the Ernest and Cranmer Ranch one winter day. His partner went back to camp for dinner and returned to find Stanley dead on the ground. It was thought that his horse stepped in a hole and threw him, killing him in the fall. Legend has it that every decoration day for thirty years after his death, a lady came to place a rose on his grave.

The large brown headstone on the northern edge of the cemetery commemorates Otto Brown, a sheep rancher living north of Deer Trail. One day Brown mysteriously vanished. His disappearance was noted by a neighbor who arrived to visit and found only Brown's dog looking gaunt, hungry and suspicious. The neighbor searched for Brown and his sheep, but found nothing. A posse was formed to continue the search. Eventually this tale unfolded: Brown had been herding his sheep when he was murdered on September 7, 1898. His body was hidden under thick willow roots bordering Muddy Creek, about 25 miles north of Deer Trail. The neighbor, confused by Brown's complete disappearance, kept watch on his dog who wandered persistently towards the creek. While the posse searched the creek, the dog retreated about a quarter of a mile away. However, when they left he would return, always to the same spot. By monitoring the animal with field glasses, the neighbor was able to pinpoint the exact spot where Brown's body had been hidden.

Upon the discovery of the body, a watch was put out for the criminal. He was apprehended while trying to herd Brown's sheep across the bridge over the Laramie River at Laramie, Wyoming. His destination – his own ranch forty miles north of Laramie.

Today the old graveyard is still used. The oldest part in the north east corner behind a small hillock has been set aside to protect the unmarked bones of unknown pioneers buried there.

SIX SPRINGS RANCH

The famed Six Springs Ranch was settled by John Hittson, cattleman and Indian fighter, in 1867. Hittson brought his first trail herd into the country in 1864. He was most likely attracted there by the many springs for which the ranch is named. It became his permanent home in 1872.

The ranch complex included several buildings. Hank Deter remembers the main ranch house as a commodious white frame, which had a fireplace in every room. In accordance with southern tradition, the main house had no cooking facilities. These were located in a separate building behind the main house. C. B. Rhodes, who bought the ranch from Mrs. Hittson, installed cooking and plumbing facilities in the ranch house. The ranch complex also included an ice house, a spring house, and bunk house. The ranch buildings were situated on a gently sloping, northeast facing incline leading down towards the Middle Bijou Creek. Just to the north of the living quarters stood a wooden barn and extensive corrals and sheds. The ranch was headquarters for the largest cattle operation of the time.

On December 25, 1880 Hittson was thrown from his wagon while crossing the railroad tracks and was killed. Within the next five years his wife sold the ranch to an Englishman, C. B. Rhodes, and moved to Denver. Rhodes renamed the ranch the White Ranch, because of the large, painted white, southern style house.

Of the extensive complex, today a single building remains, the barn. By present standards the barn seems small. However, it was large for its day. Its hand pegged frame is now completely covered with corrugated metal to protect it from the weather. Foundations are still visible underneath the cottonwoods south of the barn. Under one old tree stands the corner of a stone building. Deter identified this as the spring house. On the slope uphill (Northwest) from the ranch buildings one can see the faint outlines of the original dugout in which Hittson and his men lived when they used the well-watered campsite in the early 1860's.

CATTLE COUNTRY

The discovery of the capabilities of the Deer Trail area for grazing purposes was accidental. Deer Trail stockmen learned early in their use of the plains that the results of allowing the cattle to run at will were extremely profitable. Colorado grasses, the Gramma, the Buffalo, and the Bunch, started about the first of May, grew until the later part of July and cured as it stood on the ground.

Finis P. Ernest came to Colorado in 1875 from New Mexico, where he had in four years gathered a herd of 6,800 head. He bought enough water front at Deer Trail to control practically 1,500 acres. In 1884 he sold $200,000 worth of beef cattle and declined an offer of $850,000 for all his holdings. At this time "mavericking"[1] and cattle stealing was indulged in to a very great extent.

In those days the country was open from Montana to Texas, and cattle soon roamed at will. It was not unusual to find cattle 200 miles from their usual range after some of the spring blizzards. One of the results of this open country was the reckless branding of mavericks. This soon brought about legislation, which for some time made the "maverick" property of the State.

It was not long before there was a "code of honor" with reference to these unbranded calves, for the work of the range soon became organized. In the days of the big roundups, from April to June, required seven cowboys for every 5,000 cattle. During September and October when cattle were gathered for market, calves, if found unbranded, were given the same brand as was on it's mother. The cattle kings and cowboys became very particular on this point of honor.

Following the days of the open country, in the 1880s, the large outfits began to fence large pastures and tried to improve the quality of cattle by using purebred bulls. Special reports made by agents of the general land office in 1884, showed that 4,400,000 acres of public lands had been unlawfully fenced in for raising range cattle. In 1885, Congress by enactment forbade the unlawful occupancy of public lands and authorized the President to take any measures necessary to destroy all such fences. Many miles of these fences were constructed using smooth wire. Signs are still visible of some of these fence lines around Deer Trail.

---

[1] The practice of rounding up and putting your brand on any unbranded calves or cattle you found on the open range. Following the Civil War, thousands of head of longhorns roamed the open range of Texas, because their owners had been called away to fight in the war, most to never return. These "mavericks" were rounded up, branded and trailed to Colorado (and other places), and were the first large cattle herds in this country.

After the blizzards and hard winter of 1885-86, which thinned the herds to one-half or less, causing some of the big outfits to quit business. A wave of settlement came in, destroying about half of the open range for the big cattle companies. Stockmen saw this fencing proposition as the doom of the range, and many lost access to the main watering places for their cattle. These large outfits quit business and were succeeded by ranches with smaller herds of better quality and breeding, which have proved to be exceedingly profitable.

Some of the good breeds of cattle started to appear in this part of Colorado about 1870. Herefords were introduced about 1873 and were predominant from then on as they seemed to gain size and weight faster than the "Longhorn" on the native grasses. Since then, the Angus, Shorthorn, Gallaway, and other breeds are equally popular, producing a beef animal, which at one year of age is unequalled for excellent cuts of meat.

The old cattle trail and the roundup wagon no longer exist, open range, where 200,000 to 400,000 cattle once grazed, are occupied by large wheat farmers and small ranch operations running comparatively smaller herds of cattle.

From an article written in 1865, about this country, the writer said. "Trees will not live in the yard. Owners could not have turf, flowers, fruit or vegetables." This country was considered more like a desert at that time.

John Hittson, Indian fighter and large cattleman from Texas, was famous for being able to trail large herds of "Longhorns". Numbers vary, but some accounts credit him with owning as many as 100,000 head at one time. By far the largest cattle owner in the territory, his main ranch headquarters was known as the Six Springs Ranch. Combined with his sons-in-law, Finis Ernest and W.H.H. Cramner, their holdings controlled most of the vast territory between the Platte River on the north, to the Arkansas River on the south, from Denver on the west to the Colorado border on the east. Many men worked for this outfit, cowboys kept their cattle from crossing these rivers and becoming lost to the owners. The "OOO" (Three ring) ranch was the headquarters for these outfits and for many others, also for trail herds passing through going north, and wagon trains on the trail to Denver.

Deer Trail was regarded as the capital of the cattle country, famous for being in the center of this great cattle and sheep empire. Deer Trail is rich in the legends and traditions and early history of the Colorado Territory, ahead of Denver and the boom towns of gold rush days.

Roundups started the latter part of April, for branding calves. These roundups could have four or five chuckwagons, the same amounts of bedroll-wagons, and probably around 1,000 saddle horses, which had to be herded night and day. The same kind of outfit gathered beef in the fall, so they would have large herds of steers to guard night and day until they got to a shipping point. This is why 125 to 150 men made up one of these large roundups.

John Hittson first came to this area with a trail herd of longhorns in 1864, and established his Six Springs ranch along the Middle Bijou Creek, about 5 miles west of Deer Trail in 1867. He built a commodious frame house, Southern style, with verandas, separate kitchen, and other southern characteristics, and made this ranch his permanent home after 1872. In 1873 he placed 11,000 cattle on this range, and 20,000 the next year, and branded 8,000 calves that year. Hittson was accidentally killed in a wagon accident on December 25, 1880, near Deer Trail. The house burned to the ground New Year's Eve, December 31, 1923.

Mr. Hittson's grandson, Mr. George Cranmer was guest speaker at our dedication of the Historical Marker commemorating the 100th anniversary of rodeo in Deer Trail in 1969. It would be hard to reveal all of Mr. Cranmer's accomplishments in the progress of the City of Denver and the State of Colorado. His grandfather, John Hittson, his father W.H.H. Cranmer, and his uncle Finis P. Ernest organized the first and largest cattle empire ever established in Colorado, right here in Deer Trail, the cattle capital of the west.[2]

---

[2] In an article in the Rocky Mt. News, September 13, 1874, it tells of the opening of new stockyards in Deer Trail. It states that significant shipping out of Deer Trail had taken place prior to this, and it was selected as presenting the best inducements of any shipping point for Northern Colorado. Stockyards were constructed which held thousands of head of cattle or sheep, it had the capacity to load eleven train cars at a time. A new shipping point became necessary because the City of Denver, (which was a small town at that time) passed a law banning livestock from the City limits.

Leavenworth to Pikes Peak Express Stage Line

Reviewing the many variations in the history of Colorado Territory written by major historians, also newspaper accounts of events in the early days, all point to the most important places in those days as the gold camps. All have left out one of the most historical places in Colorado, "Deer Trail."

Soon after the first stage came through to Denver in 1858, it came to a campsite where Deer Trail is today. This was the Leavenworth to Pikes Peak Express. It came across a new and untraveled route. The stage company building the road as it progressed a distance of 687 miles. The road was laid out by B. D. Williams, first territorial delegate to Congress, who kept the road on high ground all the way. According to history, Horace Greeley was a passenger on the stage leaving Leavenworth, Kansas March 27, 1859. The original route entered Colorado Territory about the 39th parallel. It followed the divide on the north side of the Republican River, thence the divide between Big Sandy Creek and the heads of the Beaver, Muddy, and Bijou Creeks, coming over the high country south of Elbert, Colorado, then followed the ridge on the east side of Cherry Creek to Denver.

After the first trip, scouts for this stage discovered a short cut making the route about 85 miles shorter. It turned northwest at Cedar Point, then followed the ridge on the west side of Muddy Creek, following the ridge around the 'breaks' east of Agate. About 12 miles southeast of Deer Trail it angled across country to where Deer Trail is, then followed about the same route as the railroad does today to Byers, then on to Bennett and Denver.

The Leavenworth to Pikes Peak Express stages carried mail and passengers and delivered the mail free of expense to the Government. One of it's fifty-two Concord coaches would leave either end every day and make the trip in 10 to 12 days. This stage line operated through most of the year 1858, all of 1859 and 1860. Then it was taken over by the Butterfield people, later to become the Smoky Hill route, which came through about 12 miles south of Deer Trail. After all of the equipment was sold and moved to Smokey Hill, the Leavenworth to Pikes Peak Express was abandoned.

Many wagon trains headed for the gold fields followed this same route and kept alive a trading post and campsite at Deer Trail, the only post office in the U.S, with that name, the origin of which is unknown. After the railroad came through and a station was built, the town was platted by the Kansas Pacific Railroad in 1875.

COMING OF THE RAILROAD

When the first rodeo was held in Deer Trail in 1869, there was no close market for the beef that were raised on the abundant short grass ranges in the area. Cattle had to be trailed to a railhead many miles to the east for shipment to the great slaughter houses along the Mississippi or to Chicago. The ranchers eagerly awaited the coming of the Iron Horse through the area as the Kansas Pacific Railroad announced that they expected to complete the track from Kansas City to Denver in 1870.

Prosperity would come with the railroad; the track laying crews and the maintenance crews to follow would bring money to the area. Cattle could be loaded close to the ranch, and the time and expense of long trail drives could be forgotten. Mail would travel surely and fast, manufactured goods from the East would become more plentiful. The telegraph lines that accompanied the tracks gave quick communication with the rest of the world. When the railroad arrived the town would no longer be an isolated island in a sea of wilderness; Deer Trail would become a link in the chain of civilization across the Western Frontier.

The Kansas Pacific Railroad, (later became the Union Pacific), tracks entered Colorado four miles west of Weskan, Kansas January 25, 1870. On May 26th another crew started from Denver to meet the rapidly approaching rails from the East. The track moved quickly westward, Limon was reached July 11, Agate on July 24, and one week later on July 31 the iron rails ran along the East Bijou Creek at Deer Trail. A bridge spanned this normally dry creek two miles north of town. Railroad men say that violent floods have destroyed this bridge five times in the past 100 years.

On the evening of August 14, 1870, the two track-laying crews could see the smoke from each other's campfires, they were ten miles apart. The two crews started at sun-up the next morning and worked at a feverish pace for nine hours until the two tracks met at 3:00 p.m., 3,812 feet east of the depot in Strasburg, August 15, 1870. One could now travel in comfort from the boomtown of Denver to Kansas City and points east. The wild prairie was now a little tamer.

During the building and first few years of the railroad in Colorado, many interesting events were recorded. Indians attacked people along the line at several points. In 1870 Indian raiders killed thirty men between Kit Carson and Limon. After this attack, the track workers were armed and General Forsythe was charged with the duty to punish the raiders. The Indians were chased north and didn't seriously challenge the progress of the rails at any other time.

In November 1870, just four months after the track was completed a plains blizzard closed the line for two weeks. The passengers and crews on the four stranded trains ate buffalo meat and were kept warm by buffalo hides. As a result of this incident, Congress in April 1871, passed a law designed to slow the indiscriminate slaughter of the bison. The law, of course, was too late to save the huge herds of the beast.

One interesting law was passed by Territorial Legislature as a result of the railroads crossing rangeland. In 1872 a system of payments was established for livestock killed by trains; a Texas yearling cost $7, a two year old $12, and one over three years $16. American critters cost more; yearlings $12, two year olds $22, and a three year old $30.

The railroad left its mark on Deer Trail, the early history of the town was greatly influenced by the Iron Horse and in later years the payroll was important to the existence of Deer Trail. A sad commentary on the present state of railroads is the fact that 99 years after the passage of the Kansas Pacific Railroad through town, the depot has been permanently closed.

COWBOYS AND HOMESTEADERS

Between the Missouri River and the mountains were plains and semi-arid regions in vast reaches suitable for grazing. In this scene the far-famed cowboy was to become the hero.

Great herds of longhorn cattle were raised in Texas and as spring came, each year they were driven northward across the plains. In a single year it was estimated that nearly one million head of these longhorns were moved out of Texas to the north by four thousand cowboys, supplied by thirty thousand horses.

They used public lands without paying for the privilege, often waging war over the possession of range and water. The cowboy days of glory soon faded. With the coming of the homesteader he lost this large liberty, for the homesteaders and land companies fenced the plains with endless miles of barbed wire.

Stock raising was to be done mainly in small herds, using pastures, and wintering close to corrals, ending the use of the cowboy. His breed seemed to have deteriorated, and filled with men who worked as ranch hands rather than for love of the free life and bold companionship that once tempted men into that calling.

When civil authorities forbade the wearing of side arms in nearly all towns in grazing country, the fact is, the old-time cowboy is gone. Nobody shoots up the towns any more.

The first pioneers settled here as a result of sore-footed oxen or other troubles of wagon trains headed for the gold field, and in various ways founded ranch and cattle operations, some of which became very famous. This lasted about twenty to twenty-five years. The hard winters had taken their toll, but the extremely hard winter of 1885-86 discouraged the few that were left, and they quit business.

The settlers that followed those bad years produced many of our present ranches, which were established on a smaller scale. These men brought some of the cheap land owned by the railroad company[1], adding it to their homesteads and starting their ranches.

Another wave of settlers known as the homesteaders started to come in about 1908, and all of the land owned by the government was homesteaded by 1915 to 1920. All of the railroad land was bought up by that time and most of the country was put under barbed-wire fences. These homesteaders learned how to farm this area of sparse rainfall, and today thousands of acres of the finest wheat and feed are grown here.

---

[1] The U. S. government gave the railroads every-other section of land for twenty miles on each side of the tracks, all across the country, to subsidize them for building the tracks. The railroads then advertised for Easterners to "come west", aboard their trains, and sold them the land, usually for between 25 and 50 cents per acre, and kept the mineral rights, they are still reaping profits from this land to this day.

THE COLORFUL PAST

ROUNDUPS

In the early days, the big cattle roundups were for the purpose of branding calves, or gathering beef for market[1]. But, in my time, roundups were for gathering all of the cattle in the fall then sorting and shipping the beef, branding any calves born since they were turned out of the winter pasture, and weaning the big calves, which left the cow herd ready for wintering.

About the middle of February every year the big calves were put through a chute and the horns were taken off with a set of de-horning clippers. In those days very few calves went to feed lots, they were carried over and run on grass until they were 2 and 3 years old, and some until 4 years. Many of them then went to the market as grass fat beef.

The Moore Wl roundup wagon was used for gathering most of the FIL[2] cattle. Every young cowpuncher's ambition was to get old enough to ride for a cattle ranch and follow the roundup. In 1908, at the age of 14, I went for the first time. I gathered the FIL cattle and when I had a chance, I helped the cook, who was my Dad, Phil Deter, Sr. 1909 was the last time he ever cooked, but he rode with them every year until the last roundup ever held in this country.

After coming from the Moore wagon, I was able to join the Scherrer OO wagon or the Hashknife outfit for two or three days. One fall I met the Hashknife wagon at the Hashknife ranch to be with them for their last three days. They would break up at the OOO ranch. I asked Andy Middlemist, the wagon boss, if he would put me on day herd to save "Judy", the only horse I had with me.

The next morning we had good bronco busting there. Jim Crandall rode "Old Barno", famous bucking horse he had in his string from the OO outfit. "Chub" Crandall rode "Grey Eagle", a very hard horse to ride from the same outfit. A cowboy from Limon rode a good bucking horse he had with him, and Andy Middlemist gave me a very good bucking horse from the Hashknife that had thrown some of their cowboys. We rode these horses on circle that day[3]. Every day I rode one of these outlaw horses, taken to the roundup by an owner or foreman of some ranch. It was customary to loan one of these horses to any cowboy that would ride it. That left Judy for my cutting horse.

Working with this roundup wagon took us to a part of the country missed by the Moore wagon, so I gathered cattle for the FIL ranch, Prices, Parrotts, and the Milliron ranch, and any other cattle from north of Deer Trail.

---

[1] In the early open range days, there would usually be two roundups per year. One in the spring to brand calves, and one in the fall to sort off beef for market, (usually the 2 to 4 year old steers).

[2] F I L was Phil Deter's brand, therefore the name of his ranch.

[3] Riding circle, was the term for gathering cattle within a certain circumference of each day's camp.

THE ROUNDUP WAGON

As many as 35 cowboys was considered enough men per roundup wagon; most of the time called a 'chuck wagon' or 'mess wagon'. It contained all of the grub, such as flour, sugar, meat, potatoes, and cases of canned corn, beans, and tomatoes. Most chuck wagons carried a barrel of water, all the pots and pans, dutch-ovens, pot rack and a big coffee pot, one of the most important things, as hot strong coffee was part of the West.

The second wagon carried all of the bedrolls, tents, and many things belonging to the cowboys. Each wagon was pulled by four horses. The cook and his helper had to know how to drive a four-horse team, and move camp every day, about 15 miles. Some wood had to be carried for kindling; buffalo chips were emergency fuel.

Each cowboy had six or seven horses in his string. He picked the one for each day's circle to gather the cattle for the roundup. These cattle were brought from about 10 to 15 miles distance, as many as 2 to 3 thousand in a roundup. Most of them got there by 12:00 o'clock. The afternoon was spent in sorting for whatever reason; sometimes just branding, sometimes for beef to be shipped, sometimes for each ownership to be taken to the home ranch. A cowboy's best cutting horse was used for this afternoon working in the large herds.

After the passing of the open range and cattle were confined to pastures, roundups passed into history. Some of the famous roundups were known by their wagon boss, such as "The Nelson Wagon", "The Nordloh Wagon", "The Moore Wagon", "The Hashknife Wagon", "The Two Circle Bar Wagon", and "The D lazy T Cattle Company Wagon". The last one, where all the cowboys shook hands for the last time, was "The Double SS Bar Wagon". It was said most of these men would never meet again.

The horses were taken care of by the "Horse Wrangler". His duty was to herd the "cavy", as the herd was known (from the Mexican word Caveata, meaning band of horses). These horses were herded night and day, in the early years, but put in a ranch pasture at night in later years. Two cowboys were appointed every night to get them in early in the morning. They were held in a rope corral while the cowboys caught their mounts for the forenoon. The same thing took place at noon for the afternoon mount.

SKETCHES OF THE PAST
by Henry Deter

In the early days of this vast unsettled plains country, where it took courage and hard work to withstand and conquer the vastness, the desolation, and hardships, is when the FIL[1] ranch was started.

Phil Deter, Sr. journeyed into Colorado in the early 1880s, (1882), he worked for the big cattle and horse ranches and was roundup cook for the Finis P. Ernest, and W. H. H. Cramner[2] outfits for the several years it took them to close out their vast cattle empire.

At his homestead campsite he dug a well and built a sod house and some corrals, to establish the FIL. Located on the east side of East Bijou creek, close to the confluence of First Creek and the Bijou, about four miles northwest of Deer Trail. It was about a mile north of the railroad.

Many times we had the pleasure of hearing the old steam locomotives whistling for the crossings, and many times we could hear them whistling, coming in or leaving Deer Trail, a very wonderful sound that has faded in history. After I learned to ride horseback it was easy for me to ride to the railroad in time to watch the trains go by. The engines were the type with the big smokestacks. If it happened to be a long freight train going west it would call in the flagman with four long blasts from the whistle leaving Deer Trail. The long grade slowed it up about Emigrant Springs[3], and many times I got there ahead of the train. It took many trips to get a horse acquainted with those trains.

Memories of the old ranch life from about the turn of the century to the present time seem to make the changes that have taken place unbelievable. Traveling anywhere had to be by foot, horseback, in a wagon or buggy, or long distances on the train.

Going to the country school created the big problem of getting there and back. The Price school was a mile and a half away. While we were small we had to be taken there and gone after every day. Later, we walked or drove a single horse. We were always burdened with clothes, as the school term was from October to April, at which time of the year we could have winter and summer all in the same day. The cloth overshoes we had then have been gone for 50 years now. Sheepskin lined coats and mittens are also gone. Levi overalls cost 85 cents then, but cost over $7.00 today. The handmade Heyer boots I wore cost $9.00.

---

[1] FIL was Philip Deter, Sr.'s brand, therefore his ranch was called the F. I. L. ranch.

[2] Finis P. Ernest and W.H.H. Cramner were sons in law to John Hittson, who came to Deer Trail in the 1860s, and ran 500,000 head of cattle on open range, he died in 1890, and they continued his operation for a time, then became prominent Denver citizens.

[3] located about 3 miles north of Deer Trail on old highway 40 between the highway and railroad track, there is only a cottonwood tree and cat tails there now.

The lightweight saddle I rode cost $12.00, sold by a large mail order house, it was not built for heavy roping but was the most comfortable saddle I ever used, I rode many miles in those days. The lariats we used were known as the Tom Horn rope made of hemp with a green strand in it, a very good rope.

My uncle, Jack O'Connor, would help my Dad slaughter and dress hogs and veal calves. They were expert butchers. The hogs were the whitest and cleanest, not a single hair was missed on them.[4] The head and feet were taken off and they were ready for market. The veal were hog dressed, the hide left on the carcass, the head taken off, also the legs at the knee joints.

My Dad would load them in the wagon then hitch on a four horse team and leave the ranch about sundown for Denver. He timed the all night trip so he would arrive in Denver before the sun came up. Most of the time the John Thompson Grocery Co. would buy the whole load, then he would fill his grocery order there, and after the horses had rested that day and night, would leave the next morning for the ranch.

None of the trimmings from the hogs and veal were ever wasted. My mother was an expert at making headcheese[5] and pickling the pig's feet, the ears, the chin, and part of the snout, also the tongue. We had ice most every year, harvested from the big waterholes south of the ranch, this helped to keep the livers, the heart, brains, and sweetbreads until they were used or given to the neighbors. The loads of dressed meat would weigh about 2500 pounds, and the price would be about $8.00 per hundred weight for the hogs, and about $10.00 per hundred for the veal.

On some trips he would have a grocery order for about $100, especially when flour and sugar and other items were purchased in quantities to last for some time. Storage for all of the things he got for that amount of money often created a problem at the ranch.

On one of these trips to Denver, in the early spring, he always passed the John Delaney ranch after daylight and noticed some fine looking Plymouth Rock chickens close to the road. On the return trip he stopped and bought 4 dozen eggs for hatching and brought them home. My mother had some hens wanting to set, so she divided the eggs with three hens and in 21 days they hatched 45 chickens. This was very good considering the long ride in the wagon for the eggs.

The next trip he stopped at Delaney's to tell them about how well the eggs had hatched and would pick up 4 dozen more when he came by going home.

---

[4] After slaughter, hogs were dipped into 55 gallon barrels of near boiling water and the hair was scraped off. A fire was built under the barrel to heat the water, it had to be a perfect temperature, too hot would set the hair, and it could not be scraped off.

[5] headcheese was made by splitting the head, removing the brains (which were also eaten), then boiling the head and scraping any meat or flesh off. Then you added onion or whatever else you had to kill the taste, molded it, and cooled it. After it congealed it was sliced and eaten as cold cuts or fried with an egg.

The Delaneys informed him the chickens were pure bred and registered and were from one of the finest flocks in the United States.

We were very proud of those chickens. The first hatching turned out 30 pullets and 15 roosters, and after the neighbors found out about them, we had no trouble selling the roosters at $1.00 per head. Mrs. Price took three, Mrs. Pooler two, the O'Connors two, the White ranch two, Joe Crandall two, and we ate three, leaving the one we considered the best. So when my Dad went to cook for the Nels Nelson roundup wagon he stopped by the Gadlieb Egger's and sold the last rooster to Mrs. Egger for $2.00, to be shipped prepaid to Agate, which he would do when he returned from the roundup.

It had been one of the wet springs we often had, and we were kept busy riding the bog on the Big Muddy creek[6], it was my job to meet one of the Prices and go there every day. Coming home one afternoon, I jumped a small coyote. I followed him about a mile, he couldn't find a place to hide until he got to the big draw west of where Richard Price lives. He found a hole some badger had dug under a little bank and crawled in. The hole was only about a foot deep so his hind legs were out. I buckled one of my bridle reins around one hind leg and dragged him home. He was an odd coyote, he seemed to know I wouldn't harm him. He never offered to bite or snap at me. I put a collar around his neck with a light chain on it, I could pet him like a little pup. I named him Jeff, after Jeff in the Mutt and Jeff comic strip. The only place I could find to keep him was in the icehouse, where he had plenty of room in the yard in front and inside. He liked to play and dig in the sawdust that we packed the ice in. Our icehouse was partly dug into the bank of the draw that ran through the ranch, the front and sides built from lumber. Jeff dug holes in the bank, but I didn't think he could tunnel out.

That fall when my Dad had gone to cook for Nelson's roundup wagon, our Mother was taking care of the ranch. One morning she called me about daylight, she said she had heard a chicken squawking and wanted me to go and see if anything was wrong out around the shed. I was surprised to see Jeff standing behind the icehouse, he had tunneled out during the night. Scattered around were feathers similar to those on Mrs. Egger's rooster. I finally found the rooster and he was a sight, Jeff had almost killed him, his head was covered with blood, about half his tail feathers were gone, one wing was dragging and one of his legs appeared to be badly injured. A terrible story to have to tell my Mother. We washed some of the blood off the rooster's head, but we could not patch him up.

My Mother said I would have to get rid of Jeff, but I told her I would fix the hole so he couldn't get out again. I carried a couple of old railroad ties and covered the hole, but next morning when I went to feed Jeff, he had extended the tunnel and was out again. This time he had killed one of those prize pullets. That was the end. My Mother said, Jeff had to be killed. She explained how he would return and kill all of the chickens no matter how far away I would take him. I took him down to the creek and tied him to a tree. I left him there for about a week,

---

[6] checking water holes and wet areas along the creek for cattle or calves bogged down in mud. (He was 7 to 10 years old)

then when I shot him I turned and ran home. I went back in a couple of days and dug a nice grave for him. I watched Jeff's grave for a year or more. I kept it clean and shaped up like a grave should be. One time an old bull stepped on it and left an ugly track, but I smoothed it all up again.

We got one of the roosters back from Mrs. Price, trading her one from a later hatching, in that way the contract my Dad made with Mrs. Egger was taken care of. We had the Plymouth Rock chickens for several years and everybody who came to visit always admired those beautiful chickens.

To be a cowboy in those days was some different from today. Most ranches were short of hay or any kind of winter feed for cattle, except the native grasses. The cowboy would ride through and look at the cattle most every day, especially toward spring every year. The grass was eaten short by spring. My job, in those days, was to look at the cattle every day and pick out any cow that might get so weak it could not walk or get up when it laid down. We have had as many as two or three cows that had to be lifted up every day. Most every ranch had from one to several in the same condition.

The expert part of being a cowboy was to be able to tell when a cow should be taken to the ranch, before she got down, or bogged down while getting a drink or trying to escape the heel flies. It didn't seem to make any difference how poor or weak an old cow was, she would run for the shade or any water hole or creek when the heel flies got after her. I have found them unable to pull their feet out of the quick sand even though it only covered the hoof on each foot.

Our roundup wagon always made the first camp at Ross Gilbertson's ranch south of Ft. Morgan. It camped a couple of extra days there so the cowboys could attend the Morgan County Fair and Rodeo. One fall while we were there a man rode into camp and told about a stray steer at his ranch. He owned about 150 horses but only a few cattle. The steer had been there two years and he thought the brand on him started with an F, but he could not make out the other letters. I went to his pasture and found the steer to be an FIL. I told him to send his bill for keeping him to my Dad at Deer Trail. I put the steer in the day herd[7] and brought him home. We estimated his weight about 1400 lbs. My dad had shipped all of the cattle for that year and about the only thing to do was keep him another year. We intended to keep him with the couple of milk cows we had. About the middle of February, the steer was missing. I rode a couple of days looking for him but did not find him. The next fall the same man came to the roundup to report on the stray steer again. He said the steer got there about the middle of February, and we thought he must have made the trip back there in one night. I took him home again and we got a chance to ship him to the Denver market, and he weighed over 1500 lbs.

---

[7] day herd was the herd sorted off, by brand or ownership, each day. There would be several of these herds, depending on how many ranches were represented in the roundup.

Filing on 160 acres of land back in the 1880's and 1890's was generally considered the start of larger holdings sometime in the future. The land owned by the Railroad Co. could be purchased for a low price. We farmed about five acres and raised White Australian corn, a flint variety[9]. My Dad planted it with a jabber type planter[10]. White Australian corn seemed to adapt itself to the weather conditions. If it was a dry year only one stalk grew with a small ear, but if any moisture came along, it stooled[11] like wheat and would put on up to ten extra stalks, each one with an ear, the size regulated by the amount of rain.

One time we planted about 30 acres, it happened to be a very wet summer and we had stacks of corn and fodder. A shredder came there run by a tumbling rod, which was attached to a sweep pulled by six horses[12]. We had so much shelled corn we wondered if it ever could be used up.

We always cut and dragged three or four big green cottonwood trees and pulled them up in the barnyard for the horses. They would bite the bark off and eat it where it was smooth and tender. The tree trunks were sawed in 12 inch lengths and while frozen were split into stove wood. When the horses cleaned one side of the branches, the trees were turned and they would clean the remaining bark. Some of the bulls would hang around to pick up any bark or small limbs the horses would drop.

The ranchers found a variety of alfalfa that grew without irrigation. They planted it on the bottomland, the roots would go down to shallow water and the alfalfa was the finest ever grown. Our ranch had about 15 acres of this alfalfa, and for the first time we had hay to feed all the cattle through the rough winter weather.

The Price ranch had about 60 acres of alfalfa and many times had stacks containing 100 tons of loose hay. Most of the hay was stacked in one stack yard, and had to be hauled or carried to different corrals. Jim Price was considered the champion "hay carrier". I believe he could get more hay than would be in a large bale, on a pitch fork, and carry it to any feed bunk on the ranch.

---

[9] a variety of hard corn for shelling

[10] a hand planter that planted one kernel at a time after being jabbed into the ground to the proper depth.

[11] stooling is when a plant produces sucker plants or multiple shoots from the same stock.

[12] a harvest crew which traveled around the country with its amazing new equipment, to shell corn for the homesteaders.

BRONCO BUSTING

Bronco busting was one of the first and greatest accomplishments of the pioneer cowboy, and is still a prime factor in the cattle business. No matter the size of the cattle spread, horses must be broken in order to carry on the work-a-day life of the ranch. Even before the great cattle drives and trail herds of longhorns could begin, the bronc riders had their day.

The present day event is really an art under prevailing rules and regulations.

The class of saddle horses used were the toughest in the west. These horses were mustangs. Parts of the West were overrun with them and they were known as wild horses. Horses have been one of the companions of man since the days of the cave. They have adapted themselves to his civilization without losing the characteristics of the days of the hunt. They have slaved for man, having added to his pride. As the horse becomes more finely bred, he becomes more beautiful. No man lives who does not thrill to his beauty. His companionship goes far back into history.

A few examples of expressive words of cowboys:

Broncho – Spanish meaning wild and rough, shortened to "bronc" by cowboys

Buckaroo – Bronco-buster, or cowboy

Broom tail – Wild horse

Man-killer – Wild horse that strikes and bites

Sun-Fisher – A bucking horse that twists and turns until the sun hits his belly

Wild Bunch – Horses of a wild herd

Outlaw – Horse that cannot be broken to ride

High roller – Horse leaping high in the air when bucking

Crow hop – Mild bucking motion

EXCERPTS OF EVOLUTION OF THE HORSE
by Henry Deter

At the dawn age of mammals 60,000,000 years ago the horse was a tiny creature about 12 inches tall. He had four toes on his front feet and three toes on his hind feet. We know this little horse became extinct. Then about 40,000,000 years ago another horse evolved. He was about the size of a sheep. After many stages and lines of development the perfect horse continued until he became a small pony. The middle toes developed and became the primary digit the outside toes became useless, the head became longer, the back straight, and the teeth were well developed for eating grasses.

We also had another model at that time with longer legs for running, but their line didn't turn out like nature intended so it became extinct and another model was tried. The next model, being larger and stronger was more successful than any of the others, and the side toes had disappeared. Then came another model almost as large as our horses of today. He was supposed to be the daddy of all horses. He was developed in the Americas and migrated to the Old World and spread from there to all of the continents.

Thousands of horse bones have been found in France, stacked near caves, where primitive man had eaten them. Diggings that contained bits of harness proved that the horse could serve man better if he rode and used him for something besides food. The cave man found the smooth round back of the horse was a nice place to sit and found that by training him he could ride him.

From the fossils of the early horse that were discovered somewhere in Nebraska, the prehistoric ancestors of the horse were discovered. From there the evolution has been followed to the present horse.

The horse is a one-toed ungulate mammal of the family equine. The horse is characterized by long hairs in the tail and the long flowing mane, and by the bare callosity on the inner surface of the legs, by the head being longer, and the ears smaller, and the legs longer than other related species of the horse.

The native country of the horse seems to have been central Asia. It became domesticated in Egypt, and is mentioned in the Bible. The Greeks were among the first who broke horses for service in war. Solomon had 40,000 stalls of horses for his chariots, and 12,000 horsemen. In 1014 BC The Greeks and Romans had some kind of covering for horses' hoofs. Horse-shoeing was introduced into England by William the 1st in 1066. It is believed the original breed of horses is extinct and the horses as we know them have descended from half-wild herds that were once in captivity.

The horse was first introduced to this hemisphere by the Spaniards in 1537 at Buenos Aires, until then there were no wild horses in the Americas. But some escaped and ran wild, and by 1580 had spread over both continents.

The horse may have descended from a striped ancestor, stripes still remaining in the duns and mouse duns. His present colors are browns, gray, or black, sometimes with roundish spots. His age is ascertained by examining the teeth. They are best tamed by kindness. Like other domestic animals the horse has run into various breeds, the most celebrated are the Arab and the Thoroughbred.

Great attention is given in America to the breeding of horses, and the Americans have won races both in England and on the Continent. At one time it was feared the horse would go out of fashion on account of the automobile and railway replacing the stagecoach. But in the last thirty years the horse population has been on the gain. Horse racing using the Thoroughbred and the Quarter horse type, and ranching using mostly the latter. The greatest increase being in the pleasure horse which comprises all of the types and every breed.

EXCERPTS FROM HISTORY

The coming of the horse increased the capabilities of the American Indian, his crowning glory, his desire for more horses and eagerness for revenge and love of fighting white soldiers. His trick was to send a small party of braves mounted on swift horses to charge the enemy then flee, leading the white soldiers into an ambush. The capturing of horses from the enemy was considered an achievement.

The Coronado expedition of 1540 was equipped with 1000 horses and hundreds of pack mules loaded with equipment, droves of cattle, sheep, and goats.

In 1720 the Spanish sent Vellasur on an expedition through eastern Colorado. One hundred men were under his command. He came out of New Mexico and crossed the Arkansas River about where Pueblo is, then east and followed Black Squirrel Creek north to about where Peyton is today. From there over the divide coming down the east side of Middle Bijou Creek, then crossing the East Bijou about where the Price ranch is, continuing down the Bijou to the Platte River then into Nebraska, where they were surprised by Indians. Most of them were killed, a few went back to Sante Fe, New Mexico.

The great tragedy of the John C. Fremont expedition, in which 11 men and 100 mules perished, was another of the greatest tragedy suffered by an early explorer.

The pony express organized in 1860 was one of the greatest accomplishments ever developed in which the horse played the leading role. The rider changed horses every 15 miles between St. Joseph, MO and San Francisco, CA, riding each horse at breakneck speed across the prairie and mountains.

Men found delight in raising fine horses and testing their quality by racing. Indians enjoyed horse racing, betting everything they had on races. By 1869 some of the racing horses in Denver were "Gray Eagle", "Prairie Buck", "Ship Timber", "Wasp", and "Shy". In 1889 the Overland Racing Assn. was organized and the track was at Overland Park. Hundreds of horses were trained on the track and thousands of spectators were thrilled with the races, which featured trotters, pacers, and runners. Colorado had some national trotting champions. "Maude S.", one of the champion pacers was owned by C. J. Parrott of Byers, CO. At that time the track record for pacers was held by "Maude S".

COLORFUL HORSES I HAVE KNOWN

Born in the sod house on our old FIL ranch on East Bijou Creek, four miles northwest of Deer Trail in 1894, the writer grew up there.

Most of the old stage and covered wagon routes, worn deep, had grown over with buffalo grass, except on the slopes where the rains, for centuries, have washed ruts, leaving traces that will last for ages. In remote areas traces of old fence lines, buffalo and cattle trails are still to be seen.

Bleached buffalo skulls and bones and the bones of hundreds of longhorn cattle and horses were scattered everywhere over the prairie.

Many of the famous and classical old cattle and horse ranches were still here, most of them operated on a smaller scale and under different ownership. The White ranch "quarter circle shedding water over a U"[1], the Pooler ranch "P + connected", the Cary ranch "three horseshoes", the Three Ring ranch, " O O O", the Two Circle Bar " O O", the Howe "H", the Milliron "milliron", were some of the widely known early ranches. Then came the Parrett "Pl", and " scissors", the Moores "HlV", and "Wl", the Jolly " N-N ", the Deter "FIL", the Price "VAL connected", the Nordloh "HN connected" and "triangle sitting on an L", the Hashknife, the Snow " five box", the Bueck "HE connected N", the Mathews "bar over I0F", to name a few.

Many colorful old time cowboys and cattlemen of those days and from the early cattle and horse ranches came to the FIL. Newt Vorce worked there, Louis Callahan, "quarter circle shedding over cross over quarter circle sheding, connected", famous Negro cowboy, and his wife Alice visited often. Tom Powell, old time cowboy, and wife, and Dan Dameron were a few of many who visited there. Ernest Fletcher "spear pointing up running through a quarter circle shedding water", came there and sang cowboy songs for us. My Dad loaned him a horse, and he kept him for over a year.

We could watch the herds of cattle stringing in for water, causing clouds of dust to rise above them, coming to the big water holes just south of the ranch. Once in a while a herd of horses would come there to drink. It seemed to us they had fun chasing and scattering the cattle that were coming in or had drank their fill and were leaving.

The first horse I was ever on was a gentle white horse we owned. My Dad put me on him and was going to lead him from the watering trough to the barn, but when he looked around and saw me he stampeded. He ran under the clothesline, jerking me out of the saddle. That was the last time I ever got on him, he was one of the horses my Dad had with him on the roundup in 1902. The horse

---

[1] All of these brands he had drawn out, which is impossible here. They have been changed to written form, best as possible. Please see illustration on pages 43 and 44 for brands referred to in this story and elsewhere in this book.

must have perished in the big October blizzard that caught the roundup on the Big Muddy, he was never seen again.

The only gentle horses we saw much of were the saddle horses and our buggy horse. Then when I was six years old, to be allowed to ride a horse was to become a true and never to be forgotten experience.

Old Blossom had to be my saddle horse. I have never seen another horse with her unusual color. She was a light strawberry roan, with dark brown spots about the size of the bottom of a gallon can scattered over her. She was gentle for kids and I learned many things about horses from her. I had to ride her bareback, so when I was alone and she would see a nice patch of green grass, she would pull the reins out of my hands so she could eat. If I sat on her she would eat a while then would go home dragging the reins to one side so she would not step on them. One time I got off and tried to lead her away from a nice grassy spot. She laid her ears back and tried to bite and kick me, so I had to leave her and walk home. I tried her again that winter, but when she had gone about half a mile from the ranch, she balked and when I slapped her with the end of the reins, she got mad and kicked high enough for me to slide over her head. She knew how to bluff me out so I could not ride her.

We borrowed a horse from the Price ranch for me to ride. A good horse, claimed to be over 35 years old, named Tex. It was known he had made many trips over the old cattle trails, trailing Longhorns from Texas to this and other parts of the west. I don't believe there was another horse like him. He was branded on both sides, except where a square skirted saddle fit, both sides of his neck and jaws, all over his rump and down his hind legs. He had 100 brands on him, every old time Texas and Western brand was on him. I can remember he had 6666 on his left shoulder. It was a well-known brand in those days. I was chasing a young coyote with him when he stumbled and fell with me. I was not injured, but was not allowed to ride him again. We returned him to the Price ranch, and being weakened by the big October blizzard, he died later that fall on top of the Big Hill.

After losing "Tex", I had to ride two other horses we owned. One was "Fred", a good horse, he was tall, and I had to lead him along side of a bank high enough so I could get on him. The other was a small black mare, we called her "Bessie", one of the best horses I ever rode. The prairie dogs were thick in those days and had holes everywhere. One time when I was heading a bunch of horses toward the corrals at the FIL ranch, Bessie accidentally stepped in a prairie dog hole and in falling, threw me out in front of her, then rolled over me, striking my hip with the saddle horn. My Uncle Jack O'Connor, "KOJ", saw her fall and have trouble getting on her feet, so he came as quickly as possible. He examined my hip and was sure there were no broken bones, so I did not go to a Doctor, the closest one being in Denver. I hobbled on one leg for a couple of weeks, then limped for 5 or 6 months, but finally recovered. Bessie was badly hurt too, in falling, she injured her right shoulder, she could not use her leg for a long time and limped for more than a year.

Back in those years, we owned a draft type stallion, "Keota", imported from Belgium and from a well-known stock of horses in that country. According to customs and practices of that country, he was 'docked', the tail bone being cut off leaving a short stub. Keota was turned loose with our native horses in the big pasture. But when the snow got deep in the winter and he didn't know how to paw away the snow to uncover the grass, he found it easier to eat sage, which caused some kind of kidney infection in horses. We found Keota dead.

Scott and Rhodes, " inverted U in front of an X", operated the White Ranch, presently owned by the George Davies family, "triangle in front of lazy V". In those years they handled hundreds of horses. They trailed 1000 head from Nevada at one time. My Dad helped them with the horses a lot of times. After getting about 200 ready for trailing to the Denver market, they found a little colt, about a week old, but could not find its mother. C. B. Rhodes gave it to my Dad, he came home for a team and wagon to haul it home. My Mother mixed a kind of formula from cows milk and sugar to feed it. It grew about as good as if it had had a mother. We named her "Judy".

After Judy was old enough she went in the big pasture with our herd of horses, so if she didn't happen to be brought to the ranch we didn't see her for 3 or 4 months at times. In those days our horse pasture was combined with the Price ranch, and included about eleven sections of land.[2]

Some years the locoweed grew very lush and was more abundant than at other times. There are three varieties that grow in this country. The dwarf variety, sometimes called Sheep Loco, not abundant enough to attract cattle or horses. The purple blossom variety, which seemed to be more abundant in those years, very potent and eaten by both cattle and horses. The white blossom variety, also called rattle weed, very potent, but eaten only by horses.

One day my Dad came home, and said, he had found Judy badly locoed, and he had worked all day getting her into the alfalfa field at the north end of the ranch. Animals that had become badly locoed were a pathetic sight. It caused a habit similar to drugs in humans. So when the animals became addicted, they would hunt and eat all of the locoweed they could find, and not much else. Judy had eaten so much she was about as bad as she could get and still be alive.

Thousands of flies attack either cows or horses and she was covered with them. We had a test for locoed animals in those days, to see if we thought they were curable. We would put one of them in a corral then leave the gate open, if they walked around the corral and passed the gate every time, they were considered hopeless, but if they found the way out, they could be cured if kept from eating more loco weed. A green alfalfa field was a good place to keep them. We tried the corral test on Judy. She walked all one day and one night, but never found the open gate. We kept her in the alfalfa field, but I had to take her to water every day, she could not find her way anywhere. After about two months, she started to respond to the alfalfa cure and come out of the terrible coma. I could catch her easily and she seemed to like for me to ride her bareback. Some of the flies could not bother her while I was on her back. In about six months she was nearly cured and becoming a regular horse again. I had ridden her so much that when she was cured, she was broken to ride, but didn't know how it came about.

_____

[2] 7,040 acres

34

We kept her in the barn that following winter and fed her lots of grain and used her all of the time.

Judy was a small mare, weighing about 850 pounds, a very good quarter horse type, and tough as a mustang. She could outrun any horse for about 250 yards. We matched her and beat many good racehorses. Judy turned out to be the best cow horse in the country. I took her to the cattle roundups with my string of saddle horses and used her for my cutting horse all of the time. She was a good roping horse too. We used her for "bell" horse on the roundup, a kind of marker system, there were 5 or 6 bell horses kept in the remuda.[3] If any of the bell horses were gone, other horses were gone too. It was also a good way to locate horses in a thick fog or in the darkness. Judy seemed to like wearing a bell, and acted like a 'big shot ' with it on. When they moved camp, Judy would always follow closely behind the chuck wagon.

Every cowboy knew and admired Judy, a wonderful horse. I was riding Bessie, when about 50 cowboys gathered in Deer Trail, to meet a special train carrying President "Teddy Roosevelt" on his tour of the country in 1903. Secret service men kept the cowboys behind a line about 60 feet from the train. "Teddy" came out on the vestibule of the back coach to greet the cowboys. He called me over to shake hands, but the railing around the vestibule was too high so I just touched his fingers.[4]

Every ranch had a top cutting horse in those days. "Steve", a flee-bitten gray horse, belonged to the Parrett ranch, "PI over bar". Prices had a good gray cutting horse also, I have forgotten its name. "Randy" belonging to Dick Price, "T six over bar", a fine cow horse, the Hashknife outfit had "Whiteman", a top cutting horse, the Maher, "MMM", ranch had a buckskin horse, one of the best. Every cowboy that came to roundup brought the best cutting horse from the ranch he represented. This made an excellent exhibition, watching those good horses sorting cattle, of many brands, from a big herd. No resemblance to cutting contests seen at the horse shows of today.

After learning to ride horse-back, my Dad took me with him when he went to the neighboring ranches to brand and geld[5] the yearling colts. I could help corral them and keep the fire going that kept the branding irons hot. We used wood for making the fire in those days. Then as I grew up I could help rope and tie the colts. I got a lot of practice at this kind of roping, and in a few years became very expert at it.

Most of these colts were raised on the open range then and were very wild, so we roped them by fore footing. That was catching both front feet in the loop at the same time, then sat back on the rope, throwing them that way. When roping older wilder horses by the neck, then wrapping the rope around a snubbing post in the corral. We had to be careful of pulling their necks down. It seemed if they hit the end of the rope too hard, it strained the neck muscles and a horse could not raise its head. They could eat, drink, and travel some, and healed in about a

---

[3] The herd of horses used by the cowboys on a roundup.

[4] He was 8 years old

[5] castrate

month or so. To prevent this happening to very wild horses, we roped them with a California loop. That was catching the neck and both front feet in the same loop. The loop formed a figure eight around the neck and legs. Another way was to catch them by the neck then throw a half hitch around the nose making a kind of inhumane halter, but used very seldom.

Paul Henderson, "P bar 9", commission man from the Denver Union Stockyards, homesteaded the place known as the Starr place, and presently owned by Philip Deter, Jr., "lazy T fell to the left over a ¾ box open at the bottom". I went there to help with the colts at his corral, the only improvement on his ranch at that time. I had to keep the fire going and have the branding irons hot, so I decided to eat some Dry Sand Oysters, they are the by product from castrating horses, calves, and lambs. Using a flat branding iron, I roasted and ate some, but when Paul and my Dad discovered what I was up to they made me quit.

In the spring every year, we were visited by the Gypsies. They would have four or five covered wagon outfits, and followed the old wagon trail along the railroad and camped at Emigrant Springs. Some years they would camp there for a week or more. They trailed 50 head or more of horses and would sell or trade with the ranchers for several miles around.

My Dad and I went to visit them, he was riding a horse he wanted to trade, and had no trouble making a trade for a good looking dark bay horse with blaze face and white hind feet. He rode him home and liked the way he reined and traveled. The horse was out of condition so he turned him in the pasture to gain in flesh. About two weeks passed before he caught him to ride. He was gentle and easy to handle and saddle. The horse had gained in flesh and was feeling good, so he bucked my Dad off, kind of easy the first time. But when he got on again, the horse turned on harder and bucked him off, and put him in bed for a few days. I could not stand it until I saddled the horse, and surprised my Mother, when I came home after riding him all day. I rode him for about two years, he was a good horse and had never offered to buck with me.

When C. B. Rhodes, "inverted U in front of an X", operated the White Ranch, he owned two horses of the American Saddle Horse breed, a tall black mare and a black gelding. He, being an Englishman, rode them with an English saddle. They were well trained horses and he would put them through a routine once in a while. "Lady" liked to do her tricks especially the Cake Walk. "Mack" was a horse of a different temperament, he didn't like to do his tricks, so he would balk and finally quit.

George Carey, "three horseshoes", imported English Thoroughbred stallions and had three of them on his ranch at one time. He cross-bred these with mustang and quarter horse type mares. These colts were raised on the open range country surrounding his ranch, and were very wild. "Belle", a beautiful dark bay mare with blaze face and four stocking legs, was one of them. I can remember best, she was wilder than any other animal that I have ever seen. If you could get within a quarter of a mile of her you were lucky. Five or six cowboys kept her with a herd of horses and took her to the Price pasture. I was one of them, riding Judy. We tried several times to corral her at the Price ranch, but she would quit the herd and get in the timber on the Bijou Creek, so would get away. Sometime later, I was bringing about 50 horses from this big pasture to the corrals at the Deter ranch, and this mare was with them. She must have become confused, she went along with them into the corral. Newt Vorce was working at our ranch at that time, being a fine horseman, he always wanted to get hold of and get his hands on "Belle". He was mending fence across the creek from the ranch, so my Dad went to get him. But before they could return, Belle had discovered her mistake of being trapped in a corral, and decided she didn't belong there. She leaped a six foot gate to escape. I don't believe she was ever corralled again.

At the FIL ranch we had a breaking cart. By using shafts for breaking one horse to work single or a tongue for working two horses. The single horses were to be used on buggies with fancy tops, and a horse had to be gentle to be a good buggy horse. We had "Mag" and "Pet" we used on the buggy, both very good ones, and my Mother drove them many miles. They were used to drive back and forth to school, too. FIL kids all knew how to harness, hitch, and drive a single horse. So when we boarded some city raised school marm at our ranch we had fun teaching her about harnessing and driving a horse.

Becoming big enough to ride unbroken horses, I rode and broke many horses for our ranch and many other ranches. One special horse was for Lewis Callahan, famous Negro cowboy and rancher. He named his colt "The Kid". Lewis wanted him made gentle so he could ride him. He was five years old and very wild and tough, a hard bucking horse and hard to handle for a while, but became gentle and a fine horse, and he was priceless after Lewis rode him for a while.

When Teddy Roosevelt was to visit Colorado and Denver in 1910. A western welcome was planned for him at Denver. A statewide invitation was sent out for cowboys to come and bring a horse for the parades and cowboy games. The result was a huge success, as hundreds of horses were shipped by rail from distant points, and hundreds from towns and ranches close to Denver were ridden into Denver. About 15 cowboys went from Deer Trail. I was one of them, and rode Judy. In the cowboy events Tom Price, "seven N E connected", and I placed second in the team calf roping. The Deer Trail team placed first in the potato race. Judy was one of the best at this game, being small and very quick and fast, so I carried five out of a total of nine potatoes for our team.

In the summer of 1913, Jud Scobey, "JJL", a prominent cattleman from north of Byers, and Jim Price, "bar over 4 triangle pointing down", combined their top race horses and organized a cowboy and cowgirl group to attend and compete in the "Cheyenne Frontier Days" in Wyoming. Jud and Jim were the men relay race riders, Lenora Mattingly Weber won the world's championship Denver Post relay race. Tom and Jim Price, Bud Campbell from Ft. Morgan, and myself were the bronco busters, any one of us would ride any horse just for practice.

We camped at Greeley for a few days and while riding around the country we went to Evans, Colorado, now a suburb or Greeley. It was the only place where saloons were allowed close to Greeley. We found a saloon there that stocked "Old Deer Trail" brand of whiskey.

A very colorful cowboy joined us when we left Greeley for Cheyenne. Gus Anderson, "78, seven eight bar", a good bronco buster and cowboy. Gus became very important in Weld County politics a few years later, serving as sheriff of that county for several terms. Gus knew of a very good bucking horse at Ault, Colorado. So he and Tom Price and I went there, one of us to ride him. We had to corral him in the stockyards at Ault. Then we drew straws to see who would ride him, and I drew him. He was a very hard bucking horse, but I could ride him.

After arriving at Cheyenne and becoming acquainted, we were asked to come to the arena corrals, and bring our saddles, if any of us wanted to ride a bucking horse just for fun. Scobey had just purchased a new saddle with a new kind of tree. So he wanted me to try it out on some bucking horses and see if I would like it. They gave me a horse named "Tanglefoot", a very well known bucking horse. I could ride him but when he made an extra hard jump, a rigging ring broke on Scobey's new saddle, so he bucked me off, saddle too.

In the "World's Championship Bronco Busting Contest", I drew a horse named "P.J. Nutt", and qualified on him for the finals. In the finals I drew a horse named "Anarchist". These horses were saddled in the open, that was some years before small arenas and chutes. "Anarchist" was a hard horse to saddle, my saddling team were two Negro cowboys from around Cheyenne, and were the best. He kicked one of them, who had to be taken to the hospital. Another cowboy came to help, he fore-footed the horse and threw him, they put my saddle on him and I mounted before they let him get up. After being roughed around so much, he didn't do much of a job of bucking. But I could not get a re-ride on another horse.

When I went to Montana in 1914, I got a job with a big cattle and horse ranch, "S Dutchman S", two brothers had fallen heir to this ranch and owned about 6,000 cattle and 1,000 horses. The First World War had broken out about that time so the American Government also the French and English Governments were buying thousands of horses.

These horses were classified as cavalry, light artillery, or heavy artillery. The cavalry were a saddle horse type and had to be broken to ride. The light artillery were about the same type, but had to be broken to drive. The heavy artillery were horses weighing from 1200 to 1350 lbs., and had to be broken to ride and drive. This big ranch owned many horses with these qualifications, so while I worked there, I helped trim and ready many of their horses to be shown at one of the largest horse markets in the U. S., Miles City, Montana.

Returning to Deer Trail from Montana, I helped George Dodge, "d", handle what was known as rejects. They were horses that did not pass the inspection process of the different Government buyers at the Denver horse market. George bought many of these horses and shipped them to Deer Trail. They kept the cowboys guessing, some were unbroken, and some were classified as outlaws. Not much could be done with the outlaws. The good gentle horses were sold to ranchers and farmers. Many of them went back for inspection and were passed. We even got some of the outlaws passed on the second showing. Most of these horses were shipped across the ocean.

I had a very good helper at that time, my good friend, the late Nat Jones, an excellent horseman. Ed Burden, ex-sheriff of Arapahoe County, bought a lot of horses for World War One around Deer Trail. One time he hired me to take five head to Denver for him. I would ride one, tie the others to each other's tail and lead them. One of these horses came from Agate and was in the livery barn at Deer Trail. The others were bought from the Stewart ranch, "L O bar", where Dave Jolly, "spear pointing down in front of   K", lives presently. Ed took me to the Stewart ranch by auto. I left with the four horses then had to go by Deer Trail to get the horse from the livery barn. Ed made arrangements for feed and water at Strasburg about noon. They were watered and ate while I went to a small café for my lunch. Leaving there, I was to stop at the Mack ranch, "MT", near Bennett for the night, an easy ride from Strasburg. But about three miles west of Strasburg, I saw Ed coming, he had been in Denver and was told the inspection would close at 6:00 o'clock, but all horses in line at that time would be inspected. He wanted to know if I could make it there by that time. It was about 2:00 o'clock then and about 35 miles to the sale barn. I hurried about all I thought the horses would stand, galloping most of the time.

When I arrived, he had hired men to take a horse apiece and wash the sweat off, then dry the hair some. By having substituted another horse in the line before 6:00 o'clock, then replacing those horses with the ones I had brought in, everything worked out smoothly, and they all passed inspection.

In 1917 I went to Gunnison, Colo. Scobey had bought a ranch and moved there from north of Byers. He had made arrangements for me to ride and represent the "Tomichi Creek Cattle Pool", several of the members were to furnish a horse. Some of these horses were green broke colts when I took them, but were all gentle by the time I took them back to their home ranch that fall. Our cow camp was close to "Tin Cup, Colorado", a very picturesque part of the mountains. I left there that winter to serve in the army, in World War One.

While in France, I was selected and examined for special duty. When I was informed that I had to leave my outfit and join a Sargent, a cowboy from Cheyenne, Wyoming, a friend of mine, and help the French with horses they had purchased in the U.S. Knowing the disposition and class of these American horses, I optioned not to go.

Returning to Deer Trail after the war, I purchased a horse raised by Brothe Bros., "R lazy B". They had named him "Max". He was a very gentle and well trained roping horse, a good cutting horse too. I won several calf roping contests with him. One time while looking for strays, I had to look over about 60 head of Jolly Ranch cattle in the Poison Springs country. When I left the cattle to get out of the pasture, I had to go through a gate about a quarter of a mile away. I got off of Max and opened the gate, but I could not lead him through, I couldn't even ride him through. I thought he must have seen or heard a rattlesnake, so I tied him to the fence and looked around, but could not see anything, but he still would not go through.   So I went back to the cattle and cut out a wild cow, I headed her for the gate. I intended to drive her through the gate so Max would follow, then I would chase her back. Max followed her through alright, but she went over a hill not far from the gate on a high run. I finally headed and turned her back toward the gate but by that time the whole herd had come through the gate. The wild one spooked them and they all ran over the hill and scattered. I was over an hour getting them back in Jolly's pasture.

I sold Max to Ed Bemis, "buckle or backward D lazy T connected", of Littleton, Colo. for $65.00. He let a polo player in Denver try him for playing polo. He proved to be a good prospect. Ed sold him for $1,000.00 and he was shipped to California, but was injured in the first game he was used in, and had to be destroyed.

I knew many of the famous bucking horses in eastern Colo. and other parts of the State, and had the pleasure and thrill of riding many of them. Some I could ride, others I could not. In those days it was a disgrace for a cowboy to draw a horse he had ridden in some other contest and have to ride it a second time.

Deer Trail has produced some of the best bucking horses and they were used at many rodeos. "Barbo" and "Grey Eagle", raised by the OO outfit were some of the best. "Buck", owned by Oliver Gerkin, "quarter circle shedding water over J A connected", was one of the best. A horse named "Deer Trail", a good bucking horse, raised by Lewis Callahan. The Parrett ranch had an old cow horse that decided he had served his time as a saddle horse, so he learned to spin, he was named "Spinning Tom". He was gentle and could be caught and saddled anywhere, so every cowboy in this part of the country tried to ride him, but none ever stayed on.

"Jay Anchor", a well known bucking horse, raised by Jay Benham, "J anchor", later owned by Brothe Bros., was used as a regular saddle horse on their ranch and was taken to the roundup every year with their string of saddle horses. By using a hackamore or halter in place of a bridle and then spurring him a little he would always buck. He was a very hard horse to ride and had thrown many good cowboys. It was a big joke to loan him to some cowboy who came to the roundup bragging about being a great bronco rider.

Several good bucking horses came to the fair at Ft. Morgan, "Meeking Roan" from the Meekins, "quarter circle shedding water over a triangle", ranch south of Ft. Morgan. From Greeley, owned by McPhereson Bros., "reverse K 4" ranch, "Lindberg", and "School Marm" came there. A good horse at Hugo, Colo. called "Teddy Roosevelt", I could ride him and won the money on him there.

Dick Morgan, "bar quarter circle connected", Simla, Colo. rancher and rodeo producer, had many good bucking horses, "Overall Bill" was never ridden, "Pin Ears", "Black Demon" and many others. The Beuck, "H E connected N" ranch owned "Wildfire", a good bucking horse. The Joe Connell, "J small w", ranch had a string of good bucking horses. He held a Bronco Busting Contest at his ranch every year. "Chili Bean" and "The Shick" were a couple of his best horses.

While I was in the Gunnison country I attended Cattlemen's Days, an established rodeo. I entered the saddle bronco contest and drew a horse that had never been ridden, "The Kaiser", but I did not qualify on him. I entered the wild horse race and came out of it with the reputation of being the only cowboy ever bucked off of two different horses in a wild horse race. The horse I drew bucked me off and got away with my saddle. Another cowboy hit the ground along side of me, his horse bucked him off too. My helper grabbed his horse and it stopped bucking. He yelled for me to get on him and go, but his horse bucked me off too. I did not get hurt but the other cowboy received a broken bone in his leg.

The wild horses that ranged in Montana were the remnants and descendants of the big horse outfit that operated there in the 1890s. The "reverse F U F connected" outfit owned about 25,000 horses at that time. They shipped 800 Hambiltioian stallions from France and turned them loose with their horses in Montana. We saw some of these small herds of very wild horses once in a while. An interesting thing about them was the segregation they practiced. One bunch were mixed but the largest herd were the blacks, they seemed to be the wildest, most suspicious and were very clever at slinking away and out of sight.

Far from the wild horses you read about now, none of these horses ever looked shaggy or inbred, they were beautiful. A wild horse has a warning signal, made by blowing a blast of air through the nostrils. It could be heard for a half mile or more. Over population of these wild horses was controlled by the gray wolf. They would attack any size horse and kept the old or sick animals cleaned up. They severed the big muscle in a horses hind leg, called the hamstring. This made the horse helpless. They also did the same thing to cattle, generally just for practice. Horse meat being the favorite menu of the wolf.

BEGINNING OF BRANDS

Sacred things of the West, to a cowboy, are horses, saddles, spurs, boots, ropes, stories, and friends. The most sacred thing belonging to a cowboy or cattleman, however, is his own recorded brand, which in most cases has no duplication.

The idea of branding for identification, by using a hot iron, originated far back in history[1], but was used very little until the large cattle ranches of the West came into being. Open range grazing, with many cattle owners running cattle in the same vast areas, made branding necessary to keep track of the cattle and keep the peace.

Brands are made by using numbers, any of the letters of the alphabet, and hundreds of other characters. When the brand is burned on the hides of cattle and horses, it remains throughout their lives.

House Bill No. 95, by Mr. Turney, an act to provide for the branding and marking of livestock, for taxing brands and marks, and for the recording of brands and marks, to prevent the defacing of brands and marks[2], to provide penalties for violating thereof, and to repeal all acts and parts of acts in conflict herewith, was passed at the 12th General Assembly of the State of Colorado, approved April 6, 1899.[3]

---

[1] there is evidence that livestock branding may have been practiced in Egypt in 2000 B.C. It was brought to the United States by the Spaniards in the 16th Century.

[2] the defacing of brands was a widespread problem during open range days and before brand inspection laws were passed. It was done by adding to or changing a brand to make it look like your own, usually with a "running iron", a short branding iron that could be carried on a saddle, usually just a short bar or ring, which could be used to make many simple alterations.

[3] By 1899, ranchers in Colorado had been branding their cattle for more than 35 years. So the important part of this law was setting penalties for violations, and taxing each owner of a brand to help pay for the enforcement of these brand laws.

5☐ five box SNOW RANCH	T6 T six over a bar DICK PRICE	LO — L O bar strung STEWART
�686;E N H E connected, N BUECK	MMM three Ms strung MAHER	↓K spear pointing down in front of K DAVE JOLLY
IOF bar over I O F MATHEWS	P-9 P bar 9 strung PAUL HENDERSON	W< W lazy V W.A. BRAIDEN RANCH
quarter circle shedding over a cross, over quarter circle shedding water, stacked LOUIS CALLAHAN	lazy T fell left over a 3/4 box open at the bottom PHILIP DETER, JR.	spear pointing up running through a quarter circle shedding water ERNEST FLETCHER
WI W I over a bar MOORE	7E seven N E connected TOM PRICE	D⊣ D lazy T D LAZY T CATTLE CO.
∩X inverted U in front of an X RHODES	4▽ bar over four triangle, pointing down JIM PRICE	T sitting on a box FRANK FROST
△< triangle in front of lazy V GEORGE DAVIES	78 seventy eight over a bar GUS ANDERSON	S I S I connected (stacked) DUTCHMAN S
JJL J J L strung JUD SCOBEY	d printed little D GEORGE DODGE	quarter circle shedding water over a U WHITE RANCH

P cross connected POOLER	V A L connected PRICE	reverse K, four PHERESON BROTHERS
three horseshoes strung CARY RANCH	H N connected NORDLOH	J anchor JAY BENHAM
three ring JOHN HITTSON	triangle sitting on an L NORDLOH	bar quarter circle connected DICK MORGAN
two circle bar TWO CIRCLE BAR RANCH	hashknife HASHKNIFE RANCH	J lazy three pointing up JOE CONNELL
milliron MILLIRON RANCH	R lazy B BROTHE BROTHERS	reverse F, U F connected
quarter circle shedding water over a triangle MEEKINS	buckle on backward or backward D, T connected ED BEMIS	quarter circle shedding water over J A connected OLIVER GERKIN
scissors PARRETT	standing slash	camp stool NOLAND BROTHERS
N bar N HAP JOLLY	P I over bar PARRETT	toy wagon SOUTHERN BRAND

The following two stories are not written by Henry, but he took them from magazine and newspaper articles, to tell the official story of Rodeo in Deer Trail. The first is from "Field and Farm" magazine in 1889. The second is from the Deer Trail Tribune, 1913.

RODEO IN DEER TRAIL

Rodeo has been with Deer Trail a long time. Taken from "Field and Farm" for July 8, 1889, this account was also given in the "Colorado Magazine", of the first rodeo ever held.

One of the 'classic' chronicles of an inter-camp cowboy competition is the bronco busting contest, held on July 4, 1869, at Deer Trail, Colorado.

The boys had gathered at Deer Trail thirty years ago the fourth of this month and decided upon a little celebration in the way of a bronco-busting contest. They were the best horsemen in the state, and they were out to do one another up in the contest or die. The old cattlemen grinned as they watched the younger ones fooling around, and wondered, as they looked at the kicking and bucking nags in the pen, just how many of the boys were going to be laid up before the day was over. The prize was a suit of clothes, and the conditions were that the horses should be ridden with a slick saddle, which means that the saddle must be free from the roll usually tied across the horse, that the stirrups must not be tied under the horse, and that the rider must not wear spurs.

Those in charge made no secret of the fact that all the horses they had were outlawed horses, which it had been impossible to break, and the conditions made it dangerous riding. Many of the boys shook their heads, but Will Goff, a slim, young cow puncher from the Bijou jumped out and said he'd ride anything with hair on it. A quiet looking bay pony was cautiously led out. "I'll ride," said Goff, and amid great applause, he pulled off his coat, threw his suspenders aside, took a reef in his belt, and with one bound, landed on the bay's back. Swish; and his felt hat whistled through the air and caught the broncho across the side of the head. The pony hitched violently for fifty yards, making about 800 revolutions to the minute. Then he started to run, and the crowd howled. "Give me my spurs and I'll make him pitch," yelled Goff, and they did give him his spurs, and he cut the pony to bits, but the exhibition was not satisfactory. The rider had too easy a time.

Drury Grogan, the pride of the Arickaree tackled a little sorrel of the Camp Stool brand next. The animal was a notorious outlaw and had never been ridden. As soon as Drury was on its back, it began to pitch with saddle cinched. This was a direct violation of the rules, but the sorrel, evidently, had no respect for the conditions of the contest. It plunged and kicked, jumped into the air, and made a seesaw, but Drury held on and was marked down as a successful rider, amid cheering. Emlinie Gardenshire, of the Milliron ranch, was the next rider. Gardenshire let it be known that he wanted the worst animal in the pen, and he got it in the shape of a bay, from the Hashknife ranch, known throughout the section as the Montana Blizzard.

Gardenshire, rawhide whip in hand, crawled aboard cautiously, and once firm in his seat, began to larrup the bay unmercifully. A sight followed which tickled the spectators hugely. The Englishman rode with hands free and kept plying his whip constantly. There was a frightful mix-up of cowboy and horse, and Gardenshire refused to be unseated. For fifteen minutes the bay bucked, pawed, and jumped from side to side, then amid cheers, the mighty Blizzard succumbed, and Gardenshire rode him around the circle at a gentle gallop. It was a magnificent piece of horsemanship, and the suit of clothes, together with the title "Champion Bronco Buster of the Plains," went to the lad from the Milliron ranch.

Although there were undoubtedly many rodeos and bucking contests held in the era of the 1869 rodeo, this being the chief entertainment and sport of the predominately "cowboy" population of the area at that time. The next one written up in a newspaper, as far as we know, was the "Board of Trade Fair Race-meet and Rodeo" held in Deer Trail in 1912. The 1912 Tribune article could not be found, following is the 1913 account.

Deer Trail Tribune, 1913:

The second annual Fair, in 1913, was followed by the Leader baseball team contesting with the Deer Trail boys. The game ended when a 'rotten decision' by the umpire so peeved the hometown boys, they refused to take any more chances. The score stood 5-4 in favor of Leader.

In the races; the ½ mile, first, second, third, and fourth went to "Henderson" (Lee), "Mack" (Scobey), "Budweiser" (Chub Crandall), and "Waite (Bishop).

Pony race; "Tiger" (Scobey), "George" (Thayer Brothers), "Snip", (Dick Price)

Novelty Race; first quarter "Grace" (Lee), Second quarter "Lady" (Thayer Brothers). Relay race; Scobey, Lee, and Price.

Lee and Price had some hard luck here. "Barno" owned by Matson and Son, was the hardest bucking horse in the contest and Jim Crandall was declared best rider. Tom Price got second money and Hank Deter third. Tom Price was "Champeen" cowrider, and it was some riding, while Charley Dunfee rode a close second.

THE DEER TRAIL TERROR

NEWT VORSE

Much has been written and published about Newt Vorse. He was a well liked and colorful man, although he was considered one of the badmen of the west. At one time he was known as the "Deer Trail Terror".

In spite of his wildness and love of adventure, Vorce was a favorite with all of the old time cattle kings. Between outbreaks he worked as a cowpuncher for "Old John Hittson", Charlie Rhodes, and the Cramner outfit and others. Most of his life was spent in the vicinity of Deer Trail and Byers.

At times statements of many variations were made about him most of which were far from the truth. On one occasion he was arrested while in Denver, the offence being a minor one, he was allowed to come and go at will. Some of his friends talked him into the idea of leaving town, so sheriff Hollingsworth and his posse were sent after him. The dugout he took refuge in belonged to Dave Patterson, original owner of the Noonen Ranch, at the time. Today there is nothing left of the old dugout southeast of Deer Trail, and a casual visitor would never guess that it was once the scene of a strange, and bloody battle between Newt Vorce and Sheriff Hollingsworth and his posse.

In the account of the battle, facts are hard to come by. But stories claim, the sheepherder who was in the dugout with Newt Vorce put on Newt's hat and went out to bring in some water. The posse thinking it was Newt trying to escape shot the sheepherder down. No record of this man's name was kept, or where he was buried.

Hollingsworth knew the extreme danger for anyone venturing near this dugout, but apparently slipped up on his judgement of the location. Newt Vorce, regarded as an expert marksman, killed Gay Hollingsworth and wounded two of his deputies, but surrendered later when Colonel Chivington came after him.

He was tried in Denver and sentenced to fourteen years in the penitentiary at Canon City. He was later pardoned by Governor Routt. While he was an inmate at Colorado Penitentiary, no record was kept except his numbers, which were C.S.P. #3365 and #1714.

His second sentence was for shooting up the town of Evans and humiliating the sheriff from Greeley, Colo.

Until a month before his death he worked for Frank Cuykendall at Roggen, Colo. Newt died at the age of 92 at his home at 1966 Pearl St., in Denver.

Along with the above story written by Henry Deter, also in his papers was found a newspaper clipping about the death of Newt Vorce. It is a very crumpled, torn, and yellowing clipping from one of the Denver papers, but unfortunately has no date on it. It was probably the late 1920s or early 1930s, because of his Civil War service. It is presumed that the story was related to the reported by Vorce's widow or family, as it doesn't mention the killing of Gay Hollingsworth or the time he spent in the penitentiary.

DEATH CLOSES CAREER OF NEWTON VORCE WHO WAS NOTED PLAINSMAN

With the death of Newton Vorce, 92 years old, at his home at 1966 Pearl St., one of the more picturesque of the early-day frontiersmen and gun fighters whose exploits helped make history when the west was young, has passed over the great divide.

Vorce came to Colorado in the early sixties[1] after having served in the Civil War with Mosby's gorillas. He had been here but a few months when his courage in "gun play" became a by-word.

Most of his life was spent in the vicinity of Deer Trail and Byers. For the first few years of his career in Colorado his exuberant spirits found outlet in fighting Indians.

In 1887 he was arrested for a minor offense and was confined in the Arapahoe County jail. Jail life proved irksome, and, besides, he had made a previous engagement to call on a girl at Deer Trail, so he kicked a hole through the jail wall, helped himself to pistols from the sheriff's office, mounted a horse and rode away to keep his engagement.

TWO HORSES SHOT FROM UNDER HIM

The sheriff organized a posse to escort Vorce back again. In the running battle which ensued, Vorce had two horses shot from under him, but fought off the entire posse and escaped.

Colonel Chivington then organized another posse. Vorce knew they were coming, but declined to be put to flight. He was cornered in a prairie dugout. For hours Vorce stood off the party, until Colonel Chivington hurled a stick of dynamite on the roof of the dugout, then Vorce emerged, a gun in each hand spitting fire. But this time he was captured.

Several years later Vorce rode into the town of Evans and shot it up. One of the new acetylene street signs, of which the town was very proud, was smashed by a bullet. The populace poured out of the houses, armed with pistols and revolvers. But Vorce had made no attempt to flee. Instead, he rode back through the main street, shooting as he rode.

Vorce was a believer in restricting foreign immigration to Colorado. In May 1905, he happened upon a carload of Greek section hands on a side-track near Byers. He walked into the car and "shot it up".

---

[1] 1860s, of course.

48

FEARED BY THOSE WHO SAUGHT HIM

By that time that his reputation had become such that sheriffs of the community no longer made strenuous efforts to capture him. The following September he walked into a saloon in Byers. "Lon" Smith, and old time saloon keeper of much renown[2], knowing that Vorce was wanted, drew a pistol and "covered" him. Knowing that he was face to face with death if he made a move, Vorce nevertheless drew his own gun to give battle. But an instant later a commercial traveler, who had crept up behind him, brought a chair crashing down on his head, and he dropped to the floor unconscious. He was brought to Denver, but as foreign labor wasn't popular with Colorado juries, he was soon back in his old haunts.

He immediately went to LaSalle to celebrate. He happened upon the station agent, Fred Norecross, new president of the Greeley Chamber of Commerce. With a revolver in each hand, in the true wild west style, he forced Norecross to dance a jig on his own platform. The populace there threatened to call the sheriff from Greeley. Vorce said all right – he'd wait. Several hours later the sheriff, at the head of a big posse, rode into LaSalle.

Vorce was hiding behind a cottonwood tree. He "covered" the sheriff and his posse and disarmed them all. Then he mounted the horse of one deputy and drove the sheriff and the remainder of the posse back to Greeley. He forced them to submit to the indignity of being driven through the streets of the town, while he rode behind them flourishing his weapons.

RUSE ENABLED HIM TO ESCAPE

But the posse got more guns and started out after him again. They cornered him in another dugout in the bad lands some miles from the city.

The dugout belonged to a sheepherder. When the posse opened fire, Vorce dressed the sheepherder in his own clothes and forced him to leave the dugout. While the posse was pursuing the sheepherder, whom they believed to be Vorce, Vorce himself escaped in the opposite direction.[3]

In spite of his wildness and love of adventure, Vorce was a favorite with all the old cattle kings. Between outbreaks, he worked as a cowpuncher for "Old Bill" Hittson, Charlie Rhodes, the Cranmer outfit and others. Until a month before his death he worked for Frank Cuykendall, a rancher of Roggen, Colorado.

He is survived by his widow, Ida Vorce, whom he married at Roggen when he was eighty years old.

---

[2] This is presumed to be Lon Sniff, a well known saloon keeper in Deer Trail during that era. No information is known of a saloon in Byers or a saloon keeper named Smith.

[3] Apparently, they did eventually catch up to him, as this incident caused him to serve a second sentence in the Penitentiary at Canon City.

"JACK THE RIPPER"

During the early days a man of dubious character periodically roamed the Deer Trail area. Known to all as "Jack the Ripper". He didn't try to hide the fact that he wore a well loaded money belt, and had an ever ready pistol to safeguard it.

One night he happened to be at the Guy Morris ranch and instead of traveling all the way into town he accepted Morris' invitation to spend the night. As it turned out, he was instructed to share a room already occupied by the hired man, Allie Nelson. Nelson possessed a natural scowl and an unnatural glass eye, as the result of an earlier accident.

Now the factors alone did not constitute a catastrophe, but when you combine Jack-the-ripper's suspicious nature, and the sleeping Allie Nelson's non-blinkable glass eye in the same semi-darkened bedroom, catastrophes do have a way of developing.

The next morning Guy Morris inquired about his guest's obvious lack of restfullness, only to be blasted with a heated array of colorful profanity. "I didn't sleep a wink", Jack-the-ripper snorted between swear words. "How could I, when that other jasper stayed awake all night staring at me?"

THE EXPERT CATTLE THIEF

You have read wild stories about a man being saved from a long jail sentence, when it was discovered that a bird called the "camp robber" was the real thief. Every ranch in the west owned some kind of an animal that learned different ways of traveling about the ranch. Some horses could pick all the fasteners and open most of the gates. A hog or cow always knew some kind of a trick. An old hen that slipped through an open door and laid an egg on one of the beds, and was back every day after that, and would wait an hour or more to be let in again.

Tom and I owned a cow that was the best thief I have ever heard of. I bought this half Guernsey and Hereford heifer at a farm sale and in about a week she had given birth to a well-marked Hereford calf. She was in the pasture with some other cows that were having calves too. In a few days she had taken the calf away from another cow. I had to take them to the corrals to keep them separated.

We decided to experiment with her idea. So we put her in Dick Price's pasture where his cows were calving. In a few days he called and said, one of our cows had come there and had twins. She had stolen one of his calves. We got her home and put the calf on another cow, and put my cow in the Walker ranch pasture with their spring calves. When they got ready to brand they called and said, they had put my cow and twin calves in their south pasture. I got her home again and put the new calf on another cow. The only ranch left with unbranded calves was Pete Byrnes, so we put her with his cows and small calves. He called one day and said, he had a stray cow with twin calves. Pete couldn't read brands very good and wanted me to come and look at her. We took her home again and took the calf off her then returned her to Pete's pasture. Pete didn't watch his cattle very well so a couple of weeks passed before he noticed the cow was back. He called again, but said he didn't think the calves she had were twins, one of them looked like a yearling.

The next spring when she had her second calf, we put her in the Walker pasture with their cows and young calves. She only had time to steal two of their calves before branding time.

We decided she had done enough stealing in those two years, so we kept her in our pasture the rest of the summer, but in the early fall she got in the Walker pasture again. So when they weaned their calves they couldn't figure out how she could have twins, one with our brand and one with their brand. They became suspicious of the cow always having twins, so we had to sell her. I often wondered if her next owner used her to do as well.

The Big Storm

Nels Nelson's roundup wagon had been working for about a month. They had worked the Beaver and the Middlemist Creeks and all the country north of the Railroad from Limon west, and were starting down the Muddy Creek. The first camp would be at Nelson's cow camp on the head of the Muddy. It was October 21, 1902.

They had gathered about 1200 beef steers and would load out of Deer Trail October 25th. Nelson had been in Deer Trail and ordered 75 cattle cars. The day had been cloudy and colder, some of the cowboys predicted rain or snow.

Towards evening it started to snow. These cattle had to be night herded and three men were to stand guard in two-hour shifts. About ten o'clock one man came in and reported the cattle were uneasy and drifting with the snowstorm and that three men could not hold them. More men started out to help, but a blizzard had blown in, so they got the two men that had stayed with the herd and headed back to camp, turning the herd loose. When they finally got to camp, they found all of the cowboys had moved their beds into the small shack.

Their fare for the next 72 hours was on the scant side. They dared not venture any farther than the chuck wagon, and that only with a rope tied around the waist. The wagon was loaded with canned corn, peas, tomatoes, crackers, and plenty of dried apples and prunes, which they had to live on for the duration of the storm. They had to eat it without being cooked.

When the storm blew over, they got out and found a few horses, some barely alive, all in very bad shape. They estimated about 30 inches of snow had fallen so every creek was full and every side hill facing south had 10 feet drifts on them. A few cattle could be seen from the camp. Most of them were from Platte River ranches and had drifted many miles. Thousands of cattle and sheep had perished under the huge snowdrifts. Those that survived were almost worthless, some had frozen their feet, others had frozen spots on their hides, which caused sores. Many of these cattle died later that winter.

My Dad was the cook on this roundup, he claimed the blizzard was the worst he had ever experienced and told stories about it all through his lifetime. My Mother, brother, and a couple of sisters, and I were at the ranch. The only trouble we had was finding our milk cow "Old Betty". She had come home and stood on the west side of the cattle shed, the storm came in from the northeast and had drifted out around our cow. She was standing in some snow but was in good shape considering the violence of the storm. We had to shovel a trench for her to get through the huge drift that surrounded her. It was a day or two before a couple of our horses came home. I caught "Old Blossom" and rode out to some cattle we could see standing on the hills.

It was about a week before my Dad came home. He said, according to estimates of the cowboys, 40% of the big day herd had perished or were under big snowdrifts. Also about 50 head of the remuda could not be found. The roundup cook always had two horses, one saddle horse, and one to pack his bedroll on. Neither of his horses could be found, so he borrowed one from Nels Nelson to ride home and back to camp. His two horses were never found.

Cattle had died everywhere. About six or more inches of snow had fallen during the early winter, then in January we had a chinook wind that thawed the snow during the night. The creeks ran bank full, dead cattle were floating away, many of them lodged on the banks, a disgusting reminder of the big storm.

Some of the cattle died because the water holes could not be found, so they could not drink. Eating snow makes a cow's mouth sore in a few days and they will starve for water, but horses can eat snow and survive.

Lonesome Cowboys

In all of the flowery tales and songs of the old west, we read and sing of the loneliness of the cowboys and the sheepherders.

In the early days when the big cattle ranches had cow camps far from the home ranch, and big sheep ranches had either camp wagons, which they moved once in a while, or some had permanent camps, where the herders were alone a lot of the time.

Most of the songs and stories were about the cowboys. Most of the cowboys implanted here from some far eastern state and had left their folks and relatives and sweethearts and families far behind. In those days communication and travel were slow.

Some of these men became homesick and lonesome, sometimes almost unbearable, hence the "Lonesome Cowboy." Most cow camps had more than one cowboy on account of the many dangerous tasks, breaking horses, roping steers, branding calves, etc. Different kinds of slow work and entertainment were thought of by cowboys to pass the time. Many hours were spent plaiting rawhide ropes and other useful and beautiful things made of rawhide. Many practiced roping on a sagebrush, some trapped coyotes in the winter months, and played solitaire with cards for hours at a time, and read everything they could get to read.

The sheepherders did some of the same things as the cowboys. Some of them made beautiful hair bridles and reins, which took days and months to complete. Very few sheepherders had a horse, but most of them had a dog or two, so they spent hours training them.

Some played solitaire much different, called sheepherder solitaire. Years ago I came upon a herder playing what he explained to be solitaire deluxe. He had gathered about 50 or more little sticks about the size of a lead pencil and about a foot long. These he would carefully place in a criss-cross pile, when finished it was about a foot high. Then he would get back 15 or 20 feet, then run and kick the pile of sticks and scatter them in all directions. Then he would gather them all up and do the same thing over and over. This would keep him occupied for a while. Then when the little sticks got broken so badly he couldn't use them, he went back to common solitaire, played the same way but using cow chips instead of sticks.

On account of having horses, the cowboys rode miles to rodeos. Dances were not uncommon and they attended the ones they heard about within a fifty mile radius. Cooking occupied some of their time. All cowboys were good cooks. They used sourdough for hotcakes, biscuits, and sourdough bread. All could make good coffee. In those days dried fruits were plentiful, dried apples and prunes were the favorites. Beef could be kept from the latter part of October all winter, beans, bacon, and gingersnaps comprised most of the rest of their diet.

The Cowboy

When the pioneers crossed the plains, Indians met them on horses from the Spanish Breeds. Cattle had come from Mexico into Texas and were ready to be moved north. But buffalo covered the plains. However, slaughter soon commenced and in a few years they were killed off or migrated. After the vanishing buffalo came the Longhorns. Large trail herds were driven north.

Many such herds coming to the Deer Tail area. Soon the big roundups began. All cattlemen were notified and assembled in the spring for branding the calves. The same thing happened in the fall for gathering the beef to be shipped east. Moving the chuck wagon and the large herd of horses and the "day herd" of beef steers was quite a spectacle.

The life of these cowboys was not easy. In the saddle from early morning till late at night, as the beef herd had to be guarded every night.

Most of the cowboy's dress and other equipment originated in Spain. In most cases the same names were retained. His equipment being useful and ornamental, his saddle, and a well-trained cow horse were his pride and joy.

The Maverick

A maverick is an unbranded animal of the "Old West", more often cattle than other animals. The word maverick originated sometime in the early days of the cattle industry. Many accounts of its origin are told in western stories.

It is easy to see how these unbranded cattle, mostly calves and yearlings, could happen to be around. They were missed at the regular branding roundups. Some of them had lost their mothers in these large herds, or sometimes the mother died, either in bogs or being struck by lightning, or many other ways.

A common sight was to see an old cow with two calves. She had not weaned one until another was born. Many times the big calf would rob the small one by taking nearly all of the milk. This caused the little calf to look for milk somewhere else. So it learned to bum. When it saw some other little calf sucking, it would slip in and get a few swallows of milk. Some cows did not mind this, and raised both of them. This was another way of being a maverick.

The Dogie

The Dogie is a stunted yearling or motherless calf. Often when the dogies were tired, they were carried in the chuck wagon. Or if near their destination, were carried in front of the saddle by the cowboys.

The Horse Race

One day, in the early years of Deer Trail, a few old cowboys were in town, possibly had a drink or two. They got to bragging how fast their saddle horses could run. This became a heated discussion, and it was decided that they would each throw $5.00 in a pot and run a race for it. There were four racers, so it would be a $20.00 pot.

The racers were Louis Callahan, Negro and famous rancher and cowboy; John McKinzie, horse trader and cowboy; Phil Deter, rancher and old time cowboy; and Jim Patterson, rancher and cowboy. Lon Sniff, saloon owner, was to start them.

The race was to run down Main Street. At that time there was a house with a real nice picket fence around the front yard that sat about where Pundt's Drug Store was for many years. While Callahan was gone to the livery barn to get his horse, the others planned how they would cheat him a little. One of them would crowd his horse when they went to pass the yard with the picket fence. They figured he would turn to the left and be out of the race.

When the race was run, and the plan came together, but instead of turning, the horse ran right through the fence into the yard and through the fence out the other side, and almost won the race.

The Burtons were living in the house at the time and were not pleased. They finally offered to drop the case for damages for the jackpot of $20.00.

LEWIS CALLAHAN

Lewis and Alice Callahan were early settlers in this area. "Uncle Lewis" and "Aunt Alice", as they were called in this area, were Negro slaves in the South, and came North about 1865. He came here as a cook with the Hittson outfit. He had been a scout for General Miles. She came here with the Lackeys. She had been married before and had a daughter. She was cooking for the railroad crew, when the railroad was built through Deer Trail. They were married in Denver, March 26, 1888, and homesteaded south of Deer Trail about 1890.

After thirty-two years he decided he had farmed long enough and held a public sale on October 18, 1922. It was reported the sale was attended by a record breaking crowd and everything sold at a good price. Everyone liked the Callahans, it was always a pleasure to visit at their home. The ranchers and farmers many times stopped there and ate with them when they were bringing logs and lumber from the Pines, as they had to cross the creek near their place.

PIONEER WOMEN

The fortitude of the pioneer woman puts her in a class by herself. No dictionary or memory book contained all of the things she had stored in her mind, ready to be used anytime. Some of the things she could never forget were; to be able to start a fire with wet or dry kindling, how to milk a cow, harness a team and hitch them to a wagon or buggy mowing machine or hay rake, and how to unharness them, how to saddle a horse, open a gate or fix the barb wire fence. She had to know how to feed pigs, calves, lambs, chickens, and horses, and once in a while a pet antelope, a pet coyote, badger, or prairie dog. How to set hens and raise little chicks, not to forget to close the hen house door so the skunks could not get in some night and kill them all. If they didn't drown or something else happen to them, fried chicken was a certainty for the 4th.

She pumped the water and carried it in and out of the house, washed and ironed and patched the clothes. She baked cakes, cookies, bread, biscuits, pies, and other good things to eat. How many can think back to these things? She cured bacon, ham and sausage from fat hogs, also made lard and soap. She knew how to cut beef steak and roasts all the best.

She could not forget the shopping for things needed and cloth to make many things for the family. She could pitch hay or plow the garden, or set a fence post in time of need. She picked wild plums, currants, and other berries and made jam or jelly unequalled.

Large gatherings of neighbors were her joy and pleasure, she had fried chicken, home made bread, home made butter, home made pies, cookies, and best of all home made ice cream.

These pioneer women came here from every corner of the United States and from nearly every foreign country. It seems she was destined to become part of the West.

Mathew 6:33 – Seek ye first the kingdom of God and his righteousness, and all these things shall be added unto you.

The following is an article Henry wrote for a small booklet published by the Deer Trail Pioneer Historical Society as part of their Rodeo Centennial Celebration in 1969. He would have known and remembered all the families mentioned, but evidently did a lot of research to get all the dates and places.

EARLY SETTLERS AND HOMESTEADERS

Much can be written about our early settlers and homesteaders. The courage and fortitude of these people shows in the history and development of our country and the establishment of the town of Deer Trail. Most of the families mentioned herein still have relatives living in the Deer Trail area.

Alonzo (Lon) Sniff came to Deer Trail from Kansas in 1882. He operated a saloon here for several years. He was deputy sheriff, acted on the town board, worked in the bank, and was generally active in all community affairs.

Jack Stewart, one of the leading sheep men in this area came from Scotland in about 1890. He acquired land in this area and had thousands of sheep grazing at the Stewart ranch about fifteen miles east of Deer Trail at the time of his death, which resulted from injuries received from a fall from a car in 1923. This ranch is now owned by Dave Jolly. (Taken from Deer Trail Tribune)

William Shutt came to the United States from Germany about 1895. He soon married and he and his wife homesteaded two miles northwest of Deer Trail in 1896, now called the Windermeyer place. He and Scotty Patterson were partners in the sheep business. After Mr. Shutt died, his wife Carrie married Bert Thornton and they homesteaded southeast of Deer Trail in 1907, later moving to Brighton.

O. R. Masters drove from Kansas City to Colorado in 1871 with an oxen team and covered wagon. He and his wife took up a homestead northeast of Deer Trail in 1889.

William Sniff came to Colorado from Kansas in 1875. His homestead, which he acquired about 1890, was located twenty-five miles northeast of Deer Trail. He married soon after this.

Mr. and Mrs. A. J. Davis came from Iowa to this area in 1910, where they homesteaded northeast of Deer Trail. Their son Everitt took part in many rodeo events in the Deer Trail area, and in July 1921, he was awarded a beautiful horse-hair bridle, reins and quirt for champion bull riding.

Mr. and Mrs. John Maher moved to Agate in 1881, where he was a railroad foreman. They homesteaded in Elbert County, south of Deer Trail in 1887. In 1889 they moved to Deer Trail so their children could attend school here. Later three of their daughters, Katherine, Dora, and Theresa all taught at different times in the Deer Trail School.

Mary Colyer came to the Deer Trail – Byers area in 1878 and took up a homestead four miles west of Deer Trail. She came from Osborn, Kansas and her daughter and son-in-law, Mr. and Mrs. William Zawodsky moved to that ranch in 1910. Mr. Zawodsky worked for the Railroad Company in this area.

Clara Cummins came to Colorado form Illinois and took up a homestead three miles west of Deer Trail in 1904. She taught school in the Denver and Byers Schools. She raised sheep on her small ranch.

Mr. and Mrs. George Lyman Lowell came from Shelton, Nebraska to Colorado in 1886. They homesteaded fifteen miles southwest of Deer Trail in 1906. Mr. Lowell took his children back to Nebraska after his wife's death. Mr. and Mrs. Earl Lowell came here from Nebraska in 1911 and resided on his father's ranch.

Mr. and Mrs. Richard Bush and family came to Deer Trail in 1908 from Illinois. Their homestead was about fourteen miles northeast of Deer Trail and later they moved into town. Other families proving up on homesteads in that area at the same time were the Joe Hunts and Ebert Reeves.

Mr. and Mrs. James Durkin and four children moved to Deer Trail from Latrobe, Pennsylvania in 1909 and took up a homestead nine miles southeast of Deer Trail, about three miles from Lowland. One son, Johnny, helped break horses for ranch work and racing, and took part in many rodeos in the area, riding the relay and roman races. He also rode at the Pendleton, Oregon and Cheyenne rodeos.

Mr. and Mrs. Jack O'Connor moved from New York to Lincoln, Nebraska, then to Deer Trail, in a covered wagon driven by an oxen team, in 1888. Their homestead was four and one half miles north of town. Mrs. Louis Coffinger, sister of Mrs. O'Connor moved here with them and took up a homestead next to theirs. Mr. and Mrs. James O'Connor, Jack's parents, lived in the Pines south of Deer Trail in the early 1900s.

Mr. and Mrs. John T. Monnahan and family moved to Deer Trail from Broken Bow, Nebraska in 1910. Mr. Monnahan had taken up a homestead seventeen miles east of town before they moved here.

Mr. and Mrs. J. P. Ross and family proved up on a homestead five miles east of Deer Trail. They moved here from Wisconsin in 1909.

Philip Deter left Indiana when quite young and went to Texas. From there to Akron, Colorado, where he drove a stagecoach. He came to the Deer Trail area about 1882, where he punched cows and was camp cook on the roundups. When he married Julia O'Connor, they took "Squatters rights" on their land before proving up on their homestead in 1901, about four and a half miles north of Deer Trail. At the time of his death, he was the oldest person in the United States still owning and operating his original homestead. He lived to be 101 years of age.

Ernest Stone and Ed Gray came to Colorado from Iowa. They visited in Boulder before driving a team and wagon to Deer Trail, arriving in April, 1908. Ernie married Martha Rhodes and they lived on his homestead south of town.

Mr. and Mrs. Sam Rhodes and family moved to Deer Trail from Effingham, Illinois in 1909, where they built their home in town. Their son, Bill took up a homestead east of town. Two other sons, Ed and Frank, both settled west of town on homesteads.

Andrew Burns (Andy) Wright, moved from Scotland to Louisiana in 1867, where he operated a sugar cane mill, making maple syrup, later moving to Texas. In 1872, he took up a homestead near River Bend, Colorado. When the Nels Nelson ranch (now owned by Leo Purdy and Jim Butler) south of Deer Trail was sold, Andy bought it and made his home there. He was known in this area for his thoroughbred racehorses. Andy was an uncle of Jack White, who left Scotland in 1904, and went to Toronto, Ontario for four years. He married later and lived in Goodrich, Colorado several years before moving to Deer Trail, where he stayed with Andy Wright. Mr. and Mrs. White moved into town later.

John Jolly came to the Deer Trail area in 1887 from Glenesk, Scotland. He worked here on ranches for six years, then returned to Scotland where he and Mrs. Jolly were married. They then returned to Deer Trail in 1893, and took up a homestead claim about twenty miles east of town. This became one of our largest sheep and cattle ranches.

James A. (Jim) Scott came to Colorado from Frankfort, Ohio, where he homesteaded at Julesburg in 1885. He was the first elected sheriff of Sedgwick, Colorado. When he came to Deer Trail in 1894, he worked for C. B. Rhodes at the White Ranch, who was in the horse business. The Scotts; James, Mattie, and Ruby, and Laura Pancake, Ernest's mother, all took up homesteads on parts of the Pancake Ranch. The James Scott's also lived where Howard Scott now lives and their children attended school in Deer Trail.

Mr. and Mrs. C. G. Pierce and Mr. and Mrs. C. E. Fox came to Deer Trail from Kansas in 1920. Mr. and Mrs. Pierce took over the Deer Trail Tribune that year from A. Z. Stirling. They operated the Tribune in different locations here until his health forced them to sell in 1948. Claude fox went into the barber business here in 1922 and this is the only business that has been in continuous operation in Deer Trail by the same person for the past forty-seven years.

The Mattingly family homesteaded west of Deer Trail in the early 1900s. Their daughter, Lenora, rode in the relay races at rodeos in this area. She later moved to Denver and has become a well known Colorado author, publishing her "Beanie Malone" and "Katy Rose" novels.

Mr. and Mrs. John Barta homesteaded five miles northeast of Deer Trail in 1914, having moved here from Kansas. He had been a carpenter there. In 1920, they moved to town, he built their home here. He also helped build the Deer Trail Lumber Company in 1920.

Joel M. Crandall came to Deer Trail from Iowa about 1885. He and Ed Beatty drove a herd of cattle from Lincoln, Nebraska. Joel Crandall homesteaded near Deer Trail in 1885, on the place presently owned by the George Ehmann's. Mr. Crandall built many homes in and around Deer Trail and was Justice of the Peace here in 1890.

Mr. and Mrs. Gideon L. Burton moved to Deer Trail in 1894 from North Carolina. He worked for a while at ranching, he taught the first term of school at the old school house, and in 1896 bought the only store in Deer Trail. They were the parents of Ethel Burton Wible, Bob, Sam, and George Burton, all old timers in our area. (Taken from the Deer Trail Tribune)

Mr. and Mrs. Charles Fremont came from Iowa in 1910, and homesteaded nine miles east of Deer Trail. In 1919, they moved into Deer Trail, where he was a partner in the flour mill when it opened. Mrs. Fremont will be remembered as an excellent cook in our restaurants here.

The George Dodge family came from Lubbock, Texas, to Holly, Colorado in 1909, in three covered wagons with about eighty head of horses and mules. George came to Denver and met Jim Scott, another old timer. He had asthma and found he got relief from it in this climate, so he moved his family to Denver later in 1909. They moved out on the Muddy east of Deer Trail in 1916.

Mr. and Mrs. J. C. Ballard came here from California in 1908, and lived at the White Ranch. They homesteaded near Peoria in 1909. From there they moved on to his mother's homestead, seven miles northwest of Deer Trail, where Floyd Behrens lives at present.

Mr. and Mrs. S. J. Hanks and family moved to Denver from Kansas in 1900, and to Deer Trail in 1908. He helped locate many of the homesteaders in this area. They operated the Oasis Hotel and Café for several years. He was in the real estate business, and was Mayor of Deer Trail, served on the school board and city council, and was appointed United States Land Commissioner for nineteen years. He was active in many other community activities.

Silas (Wes) Wilson went from Missouri to Montecello, Kansas, where he met and married Lillian Dodge. They went from there to Lubbock, Texas, and came on to Denver, then to Deer Trail with the Dodges in 1909. They lived on the Brand place west of town before moving into Deer Trail, where he and Warren Scott had a garage about 1915.

Andy and Date Middlemist came to this area in 1882 from Humboldt, Kansas, where their first ranch was the Hashknife. Jim Middlemist homesteaded on his ranch in 1900, where the present Jim Jolly ranch is, near Agate. Their Uncle Alex Middlemist lived on Sand Creek at the time of the big Sand Creek Massacre. He was frozen to death in the big storm of 1878. Alonzo and Will Sniff came to Colorado with the parents of Andy, Jim and Date Middlemist, about 1872. They were all neighbors in Kansas.

Mr. and Mrs. Alex Simpson came to this country from Scotland in 1879, where they homesteaded on Badger Creek, northeast of Deer Trail, where the Vic Middlemists now live. Their children were Lizzie, John, Kit, and Jean. Dave Simpson came to this area about the same time John Jolly came, in 1887.

Mr. and Mrs. George Coonts came here in 1909, where they homesteaded north of Deer Trail. Ezra Coonts, brother of George and father of Andy Coonts, who used to live in Deer Trail, was an early day settler in this area and had a blacksmith shop in Deer Trail and Agate.

R. E. Beatty came from the Chicago area about 1890. He was a prominent rancher in this community. The old Beatty place on the edge of town is presently owned by John Turecek.

Richard Price came to Colorado from Wales in 1884. Isabella and John followed in 1885, and they settled in a dugout north of Byers. Mr. Price worked for several years at the Miller sheep ranch at Elizabeth, coming home only every few months. Emily and John were born here. Jim, Tom, George, Bill, Bell, Rhoda, and Dutch were born after they bought the old Pooler Horse Ranch on the Middle and East Bijou. From his Welsh heritage of dealing in stock, Richard went on raising cattle and horses and shearing sheep.

Big Loss at the Noonen Ranch

April 17, 1921, was one of those clear warm days we have in Eastern Colorado every spring. The Wintermeyer ranch was having their big close out sale that day and a large crowd attended, everybody in shirt sleeves.

By the morning of April 18th a snowstorm had blown in. It was snowing in a high wind. It blew in from the Northwest and was a blizzard from the start. The snow was wet and heavy and plastered everything.

Our cattle had come to the shed before it started. After checking them, it was discovered that a cow that was expecting a calf anytime was missing. Tom and I saddled a couple of horses and went to look for her. About an hour passed before I found her, and was lucky she had not had her calf yet. I got her to the shed in a short time and put her in a stall by herself.

When I took my horse to the barn, I found Ed Doherty's horse tied there. He had been on his way to Deer Trail, but decided the storm was getting worse, so he would stay awhile. Tom returned about 20 minutes later and was sure glad Ed had stoked up the fire, as he was like me, about half soaked from the heavy wet snow.

About ten days before the storm, an old hen showed up that had stolen her nest out some place and had hatched 15 chickens. I made a box house for her to stay in at night, and would close the front every night after they were inside. When I went to look about her, the wind had blown the box away, and no hen or chickens could be found.

The storm lasted all day and the night came on without a let up. We figured then, it would last out the night. We checked the cattle in the evening and fed the horses. The cow had her calf and was okay. We carried in an extra bucket of coal.

After getting supper, we started a poker game, none of us had much money, so after playing three or four hours, Ed had won all of it. The only way we could keep going was to borrow a dollar apiece and start another game. We stayed up all night. The blizzard had not moderated any. We did the chores again in the morning, then had breakfast, and got in more coal, then started to play poker again. About the same thing happened the second time, two of us were broke again, so to keep going we borrowed a dollar again. Ed had started a bookkeeping system so we would know who owed whom when we quit.

The storm raged all the second day. We did the chores that evening and went to bed about 9:00 o'clock. We were awake about 4:00 o'clock the next morning and the storm was still as bad as it ever had been. After doing the chores again, having breakfast, then getting more coal, we were ready to start playing poker again. I have forgotten how many times the money changed hands that day and night. All the money put together amounted to $23.00.

The one thing we were careless about was smoking cigarettes. We finally discovered we were out of tobacco. I got a good cussing for sweeping the floor in the evening and throwing all of the butts in the stove.

The storm broke about 7:00 o'clock the 21st, after three days and three nights. We were all that day getting the cattle fed and breaking a trail to water. By that time another night was upon us. The snow was 18 inches deep everywhere, and drifts were 8 to 10 feet high.

The closest ranch was only half a mile away, but we knew none of them smoked, so we decided we could stand it another night. Ed even tried some coffee in a cigarette, but it was too rank for him. We decided one of us would start to Deer Trail early the next morning. So Ed said he would leave about 6:00 o'clock.

We saw a team and wagon coming headed for Deer Trail. It would miss our place about half a mile so Ed rode over to see who it was and if he had any tobacco. It was Ed Perry and he was in the same fix, no tobacco. He said he would be back by noon and would bring us some, in the mean time he would loan him a cigar butt he was chewing, we could dry it out and have a smoke from it. Ed brought it home and dried it over the fire. He finally rolled a cigarette out of it but it was worse than the coffee, he said, so he threw it in the fire. The panic lasted until about 2:00 o'clock.

We had discussed the plight the neighbors might be in, especially the Noonen ranch, then owned by Commodore Walker. He had 1250 cows and had been getting many calves for about 3 weeks.

We decided to hitch the mules to the wagon and visit some of the neighbors. We went to Compton's, they were okay. So we went on to the Doherty's, they had come through in good shape. So Ed stayed with us, and we went on to Commodore Walker's ranch, they were in about as much trouble as could be imagined. About seven hundred of their cows had calved. When the storm had started, they put every cow and calf they owned in the big shed. There was plenty of room in it but the storm lasted so long, the cows got cold and couldn't find their calves, so they started milling around in the big corral. They pushed the calves in a big pile in one corner of the corral, and trampled them under, smothering about 300 of them. Finally getting the pile high enough to mash the fence and get out.

The foreman asked us to stay the night then we could help him check the herd in the morning. Their hired men, with our help, fed the cattle ten big loads of alfalfa hay, which took most all of the day. We counted about 200 calves, so we estimated 500 were missing. The foreman thought they must have drifted away and were in the big reservoir south of the ranch. We stayed another night, Tom went home to feed our cattle and Ed and I looked the ranch over. We found about 35 cows that had perished in the storm, also a few calves. Finally we dug through the hump of manure in the corner of the corral, and found a cow and some calves. A little more prospecting uncovered enough calves so we could figure out where the most of the calves were. The foreman could hardly believe his eyes when we showed him the pile where we thought the calves were. We made a deal with him to skin the dead cattle. He would board us and furnish the salt for the hides. We would take the calf hides for skinning, and salting the cow hides for him.

We hired Ed and Lee Compton to help us, and borrowed all the knives we could find. We set a post about 4 feet deep to chain them to, then fastened a heavy rope to our doubletrees with a half hitch idea for fastening the hide, then pulled the hide off with our mules. The mules soon learned how to pull the hides off and were experts at it. Tom and I were the skinners. I skinned the head while Tom split the hide the full length of the body, then the legs.

Joe Hunt, the best blacksmith ever in the country, came by and loaned me a skinning knife he had made. He claimed I could skin the whole herd without it needing to be sharpened. He also loaned us a small grinder and a steel he had with him. We were skinning out about 12 to 14 calves an hour, then about 10 cows an hour. When we finished and invoiced, we had skinned 485 calves and 110 cows. The foreman told me later that 30 more calves and 15 more cows had died. They had contracted the calves for fall delivery at $25.00 per head, and the cows were worth about $70.00 per head at that time. That was a small fortune in those days.

I hauled the calf hides home the day after finishing the job. They were shipped by truck to L. A. Watkins Hide Co. in Denver, and he sent us a check for $1,020.00. I was in his warehouse 10 years later and he showed me the same hides worth about 35 cents each, the slump in the market had nearly put him out of business.

The snow was melting, and water running in every gulch. The grass was to be the best we had seen for many years. We finally found the hen and chickens, they had drifted to a nearby post pile. The end of one post was sticking out about a foot on the south end of the pile. The hen was setting on the end of the post where she had perished, and the chickens were dead on the ground beside her.

The cattle had came from the W. A. Braiden Ranch in Lahara, Colorado, brands "OK" and "W connected K".

The Meeting of Two Roundups

The meeting of chuck wagons at the same campgrounds was very unusual, but one fall, about 1911, the Moore <u>Wl</u> wagon and the D lazy T Cattle Co. wagon met near the Frank Frost "T sitting on a box", ranch. Each outfit had 30 cowboys and about 250 horses, and each gathered about 2000 head of cattle for that day's work. The bunch grounds were about a mile apart.

After dinner, some cowboys from each outfit were exchanged, to sort the herds. The D lazy T cattle were left in the herd, so we worked off all the other brands. Then the ranchers within a few miles of there took their cattle to the home ranches. About 1200 head belonged to the D lazy T Cattle Co. so they took them about ten miles to a big pasture they owned. The remainder were put in the day herds of each wagon. These day herds were cattle belonging to distant ranches and were taken along, and added to each day, sometimes becoming large herds. Then as the outfit got close to an owner's ranch, his were sorted out, and by the end of the roundup, the day herd was gone.

Every year we expected from a day to a week of rainy weather, known as the fall rains. They always came about the same time in September. It had been cool and cloudy all day and about the time we finished working those herds of cattle, it began a slow rain from the south. It kept raining steadily all night.

We helped the cook stretch a couple of wagon sheets, or tarps, over the mess wagon and made a protection for his pot rack out of one of them so he got breakfast the next morning in the rain without much trouble.

Our horse wrangler had brought in the remuda and everybody had caught a horse to ride on circle, gathering cattle for the roundup. Before giving orders for making the circle, Lou Moore, our wagon boss, and Hewy Schaffer, boss of the D lazy T wagon, met for a discussion of the weather and decided to call off the roundup for that day.

The rain stopped about 10:00 o'clock and about noon the sun was out, a kind of gentle breeze was blowing and it seemed to dry the mud. All of the cowboys pitched in and helped the cook get dinner and wash all of the pots and pans.

The wagons were camped about 100 yards apart, so after eating dinner, we got to visiting back and forth. Then the bragging on bucking horses, cutting horses, running horses, foot races, etc., brought on two matched horse races, a foot race, and a wrestling match. About 3:00 o'clock the horses were brought in so we could catch our horses for the two matched races. I caught "Judy" my cutting horse and Lou Moore had traded for a Thoroughbred horse, so it was a good chance to try him in the second match race.

Charles Brothe was our foot racer and wrestler, so while we let the mud dry some more, we had the wrestling. Brothe won two falls quickly, he was a good wrestler, and became the D.A.C. champion later on.

Every cowboy in our outfit knew "Judy" so we cleaned their pockets when she beat a horse they had put up. The Moore Thoroughbred lost his race. Jim Price and Chub Crandall rode a couple of their bucking horses, but they failed getting one of their riders on either one of the famous bucking horses we had along, "Meekins Roan", and "Jay Anchor", both of them having been seen at Ft. Morgan rodeos.

They had a trick roper with their outfit, so he put on a very good exhibition of trick and fancy roping for us. Then we wound up the day fore-footing[2] two to four horses abreast, running past us, the trick was to catch all of the front feet at the same time.

Shooting dice was not permitted on either roundup, so spinning the top was the only way we had of gambling. Most of their cowboys had lost all the money they had with them when Judy beat their horse, then we cleaned them for all they could scrape up on the foot race, which Charles Brothe won easily.

After eating a swell supper our cook had prepared, the mouth harp players from both wagons got together and played all of the old tunes they knew. Some good singers also sang the old songs along with them. I think we had all worked harder that day just playing than any other day on the roundup.

It has been over 50 years since the last time I was at the Frank Frost ranch. Everything has changed, Scottish cattle are run there now. I have seen them along the road a couple of miles west of there. At that time most of the country around there was unfenced, a good cattle country.

The next morning we departed from there, our wagon moving south and their's going back toward the D lazy T ranch. One of their cowboys joined our outfit to gather any of their cattle that had gone south that summer.

I think I was the youngest cowpuncher with either of the outfits[3], and it is doubtful if there is another cowboy living today that was at that meeting of the two roundup wagons.

A Cowboy Toast: Here's hoping your trail is a long one, plain and easy to ride. May your dry camps be few, and health ride with you, to the pass on the big divide.

---

[2] catching an animal by roping the front feet.

[3] he was sixteen.

THE COLORFUL PAST

THE WATERMELON PATCH

The original "Homestead Act" which allowed filing on 160 acres, required 40 acres to be plowed before a patent could be obtained. In 1910 the law was changed allowing a person to file on 320 acres, 80 acres to be plowed. Most of the homesteaders plowed a small patch for a garden, which grew the best and most delicious vegetables. It always seemed that watermelons grown on the native sod were the very best.

In 1916 I helped the Prices at haying time. We worked the home ranch first, then moved the haying crew to the Carey ranch. The hay crop was very good that year, so we would be there for some time.

I had to be the horse wrangler and left the ranch at 4:00 o'clock every morning. Most every morning I would go east across the creek onto a high hill, from there I would see most of the big pasture.

Tom Hayes had homesteaded just east of the ranch and built his house between the creek and the high hill. I had noticed his melon patch was in the yard around the house, between the house and the Carey ranch fence line.

Bill Zawodsky was one of the haying crew. When I told him about the melons, right away, he decided to steal one when they were ripe. Bill was kind of happy go lucky kind of a guy, and every time he saw Tom Hayes he would tell him how he liked to steal watermelon, and asked him to keep him posted on when he thought they were ripe. Tom told him he was welcome to one of the melons if he was careful not to get filled with buckshot or torn to pieces by two viscous dogs he owned.

Bill made a couple of trips by the yard, and made a quick survey of the place, and told Tom the melon he wanted was growing under his bedroom window, and if he missed it, he would know where it had gone.

Every morning when I passed close to the fence the two big dogs would chase me over the hill, and acted as viscous as Tom had claimed. I had to watch them closely, as they would run and jump and try to grab me by the feet or legs while on my horse.

The morning Bill decided to get the big melon was kind of gloomy, darker than usual. Bill rode behind the saddle with me until we got to the east bank of the creek. The bank was about 4 feet high and the fence line had grown full of tall sweet clover over the top wire on the fence. Bill could hear the dogs barking at me and knew I would kind of fight at them that morning. When I went over the hill, he slipped along the fence and through the open gate that lead into the Carey pasture. He climbed over a kind of low fence into the yard, grabbed the melon and was gone in a few seconds. Then he sneaked along the fence line back to the creek where he was out of sight of Tom's house, and was back at the ranch in a short time.

The dogs followed me about a half mile that morning then laid down on a little hill to wait for me to bring horses back by there. The horses were in the south end of the pasture so I took them down the creek to the ranch. The dogs didn't have a chance to chase them.

When I went to breakfast I saw the big melon on the floor and Bill was phoning Tom to come over and help eat it.

Tom Hayes was a husky built man, with plenty of temper. It was hard to tell how he would take the joke. He came over just to find out how Bill got the melon.

We kept the melon on ice all day, then after supper the whole crew took the melon back, cut it, and enjoyed one of the best melons ever.

Tom Hayes was a fine gentleman and always enjoyed telling the story about the melon and the "worthless" dogs he owned.

THE LAST TRAIL HERD, MAY 1920
by Henry Deter

This large herd of cattle was owned by the Denver Livestock Commission Co., Union Stockyards, Denver. They were counted to Jack Woods, exactly 1500 head, and wintered on his ranch about 25 miles south of Deer Trail.

Andy Middlemist called me and asked if I could help move this huge herd of cattle to Brush, Colorado, by trail, about 100 miles, then by rail to Whitman, Nebraska, where I would deliver and count them to the foreman of a large Nebraska ranch. He said Al Reed was to be the trail boss, Chub Crandall would drive the chuckwagon and cook. There were eight other cowboys. I was to be the point man and scout, so would not be under orders from the boss except for night herding. My responsibility was to keep the herd from traveling to fast and on a straight trail across country.

Circumstances made me one day late, so the cattle were gathered and counted out of the pasture to the trail boss, 1497 head. Jack Woods knew five of them had died during the winter, so somewhere we had a miscount or some strays. These cattle were all three and four year old steers and were every color; buckskin, blue roan, black, white, brindle, and many combinations of color. They were distant relatives of the longhorns, but had been dehorned, and the holding brand was a standing slash " \ ", branded on the left shoulder.

My route was planned to stay on the large ranch pastures as much as possible, staying out of lanes and off the graveled roads. Watering this herd was our most perplexing problem. We had to avoid small waterholes and windmill tanks so we stayed off water, as you will see, as we trailed toward Brush.

Plans had to be made for holding them at night. There were no pastures or corrals, so we had to night herd them. Every cowboy had to take his turn of two hours on night herd or stand guard as some called it. The cattle were wild enough to handle easily, as long as you stayed on your horse. We trained them to bed down about the second night, a very beautiful sight to see them all lying down but one or two.

Fred Matson was the horse wrangler. His job was the hardest for any of the trail cowboys. He had to watch for some old homesick horse trying to get away and leave for his home ranch. He had to keep them away from the cattle, and train them to follow the chuckwagon. When we moved camp, he had to find water for them and have them in a rope corral so every cowboy could tie one up for the night and hobble one[1]. Each cowboy had two horses. I had three, because one of Fred Matson's horses had thrown him the first day so he gave him to me to ride. The first time I rode this horse he bucked several times.

---

[1] a restriction placed around the front legs of a horse, usually made of soft rope and twisted between the legs, allowing them to wander around a little to eat, but would not allow them to go fast enough to get very far, also made them easier to catch.

The second morning I had noticed a kind of brindle white faced steer with a wattle[2] on his nose, grazing around close to camp, and again after we had started to move the herd he seemed to be following me. He would stay behind me but ahead of every other steer. He would even chase some of the other steers back. When I was stringing them out he would be right behind my horse. He did the same thing every day, so he must have appointed himself as the leader of that herd.

We had watered the herd while crossing the Bijou Creek north of Agate so were without water the next couple of days. I had to steer them away from small water holes on the Jolly ranch. While I had gone ahead a mile or so to find a camp site and bed ground for the night, the wind changed directions and they could smell the water at the mouth of Poison Springs draw about a mile away. They turned in that direction and left on a run. They got away from the cowboys and ran to the small waterhole but could not get a drink there. By the time I had returned, about 100 head of them were caught in the mud around the water. It wouldn't be hard to guess, that the cowboys were all excited. We decided to set on the bank and watch them a while and just let them alone. One by one they got out of the mud. The last one was the largest and wildest steer in the herd. The only part of him out of the mud was his head. It looked like we were in for trouble getting him out, but when I started to walk toward him, he wiggled loose, so when I slapped him on the nose with my hat he came right out after me. I had to run to get to my horse. We bedded down about two miles from there that night.

Next day we were joined by Date Middlemist who was to be a point man also. The job was getting harder the longer we went without water for the herd. We camped and bedded them in a lagoon that night, (there are several oil wells and a refinery there now). About half an hour after most of them had laid down I saw a commotion near the center of the herd, just about dusk. I finally rode out there among them and found a man on foot carrying a small dog in his arms. He was looking for his milk cow. When I turned the leader back toward the bed grounds, I had encircled him. Probably no more than 75 steers knew he was there. How the herd got by without stampeding or milling around him we could not figure out. He walked beside my horse and I got him away without any kind of disaster.

The next day a nice breeze blew from the north all day. The cattle were hard to hold back and when they were within four or five miles of a large lake at the Anton Nelson ranch, they began to trot. They could smell the water that far away. When they arrived at the lake, they did not stop to drink but swam across the lake about 400 feet. Then they turned back, waded in, and drank some. They stayed around the water about three hours drinking a little at a time until they were satisfied.

We bedded them in a lagoon in the sand hills that night, which was a perfect spot. We could ride on high ground around the herd. About midnight, the

---

[2] One method used for marking cattle was a wattle. It is a piece of skin that has been cut loose, then given a twist, which causes it to heal into a hanging strip or ball of hide.

boss came in. It was his turn on guard. He called out everybody, it had begun to rain, he was afraid the steers would get up and drift with the rain. But they did not move, they just stayed lying down. The rain was light and came down slow and easy. The lightning was terrific, it kept the sky lit up all of the time. It lasted about an hour, and as we rode around the herd it looked like a large city at a distance. Every drop of water hanging from the ears, end of nose, or anywhere, was aglow resembling a small light bulb. Our bridles, spurs, and horses ears and tails were the same. It looked like millions of lights. We found out later it was called phosphorescent lighting, and caused a sight seldom ever seen. I never have seen anything like it since.

We were about twelve miles south of Brush, so our last day would be the drive to the stockyards at Brush. We wanted to graze as long as possible and had to return to the big lake to water, so we did not leave there until about 11 o'clock. By that time the wind was blowing from the north like a hurricane. We had to steer around the blowouts in the sand hills to protect our faces and eyes from the sharp sand. The black dust from the beet fields ahead of us was beginning to fill the air. When we got into the irrigated farming country, we had to stay in the lanes. We had to be sure this herd did not get into a field or some farmyard, so we were busy. The dust got worse all the afternoon.

We had to travel along the railroad about a mile and a train gave our steers quite a scare, but they did not get away. About sundown we started corralling them. We were glad to find enough room in the stockyards to pen them all. Our boss and the chuckwagon and horse wrangler were behind that herd all day. They were a sight never to be forgotten, just covered with dust. The wind blew all night the same way. The dust had ruined everything we had to eat, so we went to a restaurant down town, and had to stay at a hotel that night. When the sun came up the next morning the wind had gone down and the day was calm.

While getting ready for the cattle drive, Fred Matson discovered he did not have a pair of cowboy boots or a big hat, so Tom Price loaned him his boots, two sizes too large, and an old black hat, also too large. He had put on a white shirt and necktie when he left Deer Trail. After a week on the trail and all day in that dust, his white shirt was badly soiled. But the necktie came in handy, the only way he could keep his hat from blowing off was to put the necktie over his hat and head and tie it under his chin.

The end of the cattle trails that have gone in history found us getting ready to ship by rail to Whitman, Nebraska. The brand inspector was called, as these cattle were going out of state. Dan Gilbert was the brand inspector, who was a good friend of mine. He asked me to also inspect this herd and also count them. When we had finished, I had taken out two steers that I thought were strays and put them in a corral separate from the herd. I had counted the cattle and came up with 1496 head, including the two strays. Gilbert came up with the same number. We had left a sick steer at the B. D. Middlemist ranch, that with the five found dead on the Jack Woods ranch made up the original 1500.

We roped and tied the two steers I had cut out as strays, and clipped them[3]. They belonged to an outfit that had shipped their cattle from a southern state to winter on a ranch east of Colorado Springs, and had been with the herd for awhile. They were branded in the south and the brand was not recorded in Colorado. They were advertised as strays in the Record Stockman, the official cattleman's paper, and the ownership was established that way. Dan Gilbert called the brand a toy wagon, (see brand illustration page).

The steers were loaded 22 to a railroad car and left Brush about 4:00 o'clock in the afternoon. I had the billing[4] and the brand inspector's clearance on these cattle. Chub Crandall went with me, and we arrived in Whitman about 1:00 o'clock in the morning. It had been raining for about two hours. The railroad crew had orders to unload the cattle, so Chub and I went over town to the hotel. We could not find any of the hotel people, so we found a good bed upstairs and went to bed. We were up about 6:00 o'clock, the weather was about the same, raining a steady downpour. The manager finally showed up and was as surprised as we were, all being acquainted for a long time. We had a very good breakfast with them and had just finished eating when the Nebraska cowboys showed up to receive the cattle. I asked the boss how he wanted to count them out. He informed me he knew how to count cattle, and counted them out in the open, but when I showed him the papers I had, he blowed up. He was two short of the count, he would not receive them that way, so his cowboys had to corral them again. I didn't think they could do it but they did. I told the boss I didn't want to fool around in the rain any longer than necessary so he would have to count them my way. I would count out 100 at a time, and when he was sure that was correct he could let them out. We soon had the herd counted. He accepted the papers I had, and the big herd was delivered, 1494 head. As they disappeared into the rain and distance, Chub and I just stood and took a long look at the last big herd of cattle ever to be trailed from this part of the country, an experience of a whole lifetime, which we could never have again.

Most of the cowboys have passed now. Date Middlemist and I get together once in a while, and reminisce about this trail herd and the many things that happened almost a half a century ago.

HIGH LIGHTS OF THE TRAIL

The chuckwagon belonged to the Hashknife outfit and had been used on many roundups in the early days. Chub Crandall, our cook, had the same menu three times a day, two fried eggs each, plenty of bacon, coffee, bread and butter, and for desert he opened canned tomatoes.

After loading 68 cattle cars with these big steers, our billing had preference over every other train so we went straight through to Whitman. The train crew invited us to play poker with them. We had bought some sandwiches

---

[3] clip or shear the hair away from a hard to read brand so it can be identified.
[4] bill of lading

before we left Brush, and after we had rested a little and ate some, we started a poker game. When we arrived at Whitman and invoiced, we were both winners, I about $25.00 and Chub about $40.00. What that train crew called us could not be printed here.

The horse Fred Matson loaned me was a small horse, weight about 1000 lbs., very quick and had thrown several other cowboys. He was gentle and easy to saddle and easy to mount. Sometimes he would have to buck when you first got on, then other times he would go awhile, nothing ever had to happen to him, he would just turn on and buck anytime, a very hard bucking horse. I finally uncoiled the end of my lariat and when he tried to buck me off, I would whip him anywhere I could hit him with it. I accidentally hit him in the left eye with the knot on the end of my rope, he quit right there. He had learned his lesson the hard way, that was the last time he ever tried to throw me. His eye got well and he was a good horse.

Night herding with only our small crew was something for the boss to be proud of. I always took the last stand from 4:00 to 6:00 in the morning, then I didn't have to go to bed again. The night of the phosphorescent lighting was so bad, and everything so beautiful for a while. It turned out to be the darkest night that ever was. Everybody got lost, the soap weed bushes looked like steers lying down, so we herded them too. The steers nor our horses ever seemed to be afraid of the phosphorescent lighting.

We had sidetracked ranches and farms so well that the only visitors we had were several small bunches of horses. Some had come a couple of miles to see that herd of cattle. A few milk cows came to see us, but if left alone, would leave in a short time. The morning after the man and dog incident, I rode over to his farm to see about his cow, and she had been home all the time. He said some of the big steers had brushed him real hard, and he was afraid of falling while among them. Another fellow came after his cows in a spring wagon with one horse hitched to it. While he was chasing them the single tree[5] broke, the horse ran away, and he was thrown out, but not hurt. We had to pass close to a one-room schoolhouse. I told the teacher to bring her pupils out to the yard fence and watch the cattle go by. They lined up on the fence and sat quietly until every steer had passed.

The windstorm was one of the worst I have ever experienced. When we went to the hotel the manager didn't think it possible to be able to handle that many cattle in such a wind. We were the dirtiest and tiredest cowboys he had ever seen. Some of us had brought a change of clothes in our bedrolls, so after a bath and shave and a big steak, we felt better and sure did sleep good that night.

The valuation of the herd of steers could be estimated at about $100,000.00 at that time, and about half a million at present prices.

---

[5] part of the harness that hitched the horse to the wagon.

DETER BARBECUE

The Deter "Barbecue" idea was brought here by Philip Deter, Sr. in the 1880s, and was known as open pit Barbecue. The meat being roasted on a grate over a bed of coals made by burning some kind of wood, hardwood being the best, cottonwood the most common in the state, is very good.

In the early days whole quarters were the easiest way to handle the meat. It was turned often with large forks. Later meat came from packing houses and what is called short rounds were purchased, weighing about 75 pounds each, then roasted for about eighteen hours.

The first Barbecue I helped with was at Hugo, Colorado. If I remember correctly the year was 1912. My Dad, Joe Hunt, our helper, and myself cooked four head of cattle, slaughtered at a ranch there. We fed an estimated 5,000 people. Since then several hundred thousand people have eaten "Deter Barbecue". We have cooked for Cattlemen's meetings, Turkey Shoots, Elks at Ft. Morgan and Wray, Colorado, Sacred Heart Retreat at Sedalia, Colorado, Press Club at Estes Park, Colorado, Flying Farmers at Akron, Colorado, Buffalo meat, Aurora, Colorado, Beef, Buffalo, deer, and pork for soldiers, Limon, Colorado, for the Cattlemen four times. Several times in the City of Denver for auto auctions, oil well outfits, and other events. The largest was put on at Lexington, Nebraska where we had sixty rounds cooking at the same time. Ten thousand people got there to eat and ten thousand more were held up by a road block and could not get there to eat.

For the last several years, I have been serving "Chuckwagon Dinners" for the Deer Trail Historical Society. Something similar to the old time meals served to cowboys on the cattle roundups of the past.

My Dad, Phil Deter, Sr., was a cook for Ernest and Cranmer, cattle kings, when they sold their vast cattle empire, on one of the five roundup wagons when they were gathering their thousands of cattle for shipment.

For the "Centennial"[1] I went to Hugo, Colorado, for the re-enactment of the cowboys serving breakfast to Teddy Roosevelt when he was touring the country in 1903. Their chuckwagon was camped in a small park near the railroad at that time. My crew cooked and served about 500 steaks and baked about 1000 biscuits, and made lots of coffee that day.

---

[1] Colorado's Centennial celebration in 1976. Colorado is known as the Centennial State because it was admitted to the union in 1876, during the celebration of the 100th anniversary of the signing of the Declaration of Independence.

The Cowboy's love for songs and poems probably began back when they spent a lot of time around a campfire in the evenings. On spring and fall roundups it would get dark a couple of hours before bedtime, so there was time for a lot of singing, reciting, and story telling. It is also true that cowboys would sometimes sing to the cattle to help settle them down at night. Besides roundups, some cowboys spent a lot of time in a bunk house or alone in a line shack or cow camp, and usually spent long hours alone on the back of a horse. With no TV, movie theatres, and only a few scarce books to read, cowboys created their own entertainment in the form of songs, poems, and stories. This probably accounts for the popularity of Cowboy Poets, and Country Western music to this day.

My Grandfather loved old cowboy songs and poems and had lots of them around, and was always clipping them out and saving them. The ones included here are ones he had copied down by hand and saved, so they must have been extra meaningful to him. He also wrote the little introduction at the beginning.

COWBOY SONGS AND POEMS

Western culture, created in the West for the West, aided by its literature, and its freedom, is unequalled anywhere. It is all portrayed in cowboy songs, cowboy poems, and western stories. It nourishes the highest emotions, to the end that dominated our lives by "God and Duty", the problems of time and eternity.

All of these have been written before, some parts have been stolen, some added and some deleted from Western historians and Western authors. It is hoped some inspiration will come of it. It is dedicated to all who read it and to remind all of us at Deer Trail of the proud tradition we possess.

CODE OF THE COW COUNTRY

It don't take such a lot o'laws to keep the rangeland straight
Nor books to write em in, cause there are only six or eight.

The first one is the "Welcome Sign", written deep in western hearts,
My camp is yours and yours is mine in all cow country parts.

Treat with respect all womankind, same as you would your sister,
Care for neighbor's strays you find, and don't call cowboys "Mister".

Shut the pasture gates when passing through, and taking all in all,
Be just as rough as pleases you, but never mean or small.

Talk straight, shoot straight, never break your word to man or boss,
Plumb always kill a rattlesnake, don't ride a sore-back hoss.

It don't take law nor pedigree to live the best you can,
These few is all it takes to be a cowboy and a man.

THE GREAT ROUNDUP
From M.S. Johnson's "Trail Blazing"

When I think of the last great roundup,
On the eve of eternity's dawn,
I think of the past and cowboys,
Who have been with us here, and have gone.

And I wonder if any will greet me,
On the sands of the evergreen shore,
With a hearty "God Bless You, Old Fellow",
That I've met with so often before.

I think of the big hearted fellows,
Who will divide with you blanket and bread,
With a piece of stray beef well roasted,
And charge for it never a "red".

I often look upward and wonder,
If the green fields will seem half so fair,
If any, the wrong trail have taken,
And fail to "be in" over there.

If the trail that leads down to perdition,
Is paved all the way with good deeds;
But in the great roundup of ages,
"Dear Boys", this won't answer your needs.

COWBOY POEM
Source unknown

A cowboy stood at the golden gate
His face worn and old
He meekly asked the man of fate
Admission to the fold,

"What did you do?" St. Peter asked
"To seek admission here."
"A cowboy down on earth
I was for many a year."

The gate swung open sharply then,
St Peter touched a bell,
"Come in", he said, "and take a harp,
You've served your time in hell."

GIT ALONG LITTLE DOGIE

This is one of the best known of the cowboy songs. The source of most of the cowboy songs is hard to trace beyond the fact that they originated with the cowboys themselves.

As I was a walking one morning for pleasure,
I spied a young cowboy a riding along;
His hat was throwed back and his spurs was a jingling,
An as he approached he was singing this song.

Whoopee ti yi yo, git along little dogies,
It's your misfortune and none of my own.
Whoopee ti yi yo, git along little dogies,
You know Wyoming will be your new home.

Its early in Spring that we roundup the dogies,
We mark them and brand them and bob off their tails;
We roundup our horses, load up the chuckwagon,
And then throw the dogies out on the trail.

Whoopee ti yi yo, git along little dogies,
It's your misfortune and none of my own.
Whoopee ti yi yo, git along little dogies,
You know Wyoming will be your new home.

Its whooping and yelling and driving the dogies,
And ok how I wish you would only go on;
It whooping and punching, go on little dogies,
You know that Wyoming will be your new home.

Whoopee ti yi yo, git along little dogies,
It's your misfortune and none of my own.
Whoopee ti yi yo, git along little dogies,
You know Wyoming will be your new home.

Some boys they go up on the trail just for pleasure,
But that's where they get it most awfully wrong;
You haven't a notion the trouble they give us,
It takes all our time to keep moving along.

Whoopee ti yi yo, git along little dogies,
It's your misfortune and none of my own.
Whoopee ti yi yo, git along little dogies,
You know Wyoming will be your new home.

MY OLD STETSON HAT
Author unknown

Stained with alkali, sand and mud
Smeared by grease and crimson blood
Battered and bent from constant use
Still you have stood the dang abuse.

A true companion through all these years
Fanning broncs and Longhorn steers
I dedicate this to the old gray lid
For the useful things that old hat did.

Used to decoy some rustler's lead
Or as a pillow beneath my head
Coaxing smoldering fire in the cold
Panning dust in search for gold.

Pushed up big and knocked down flat
Has been the lot of my old Stetson hat
For carrying oats to a piebald bronc
Security for drinks at the Honky Tonk.

Mistreated, abused on a roundup spree
Walked on, tromped on, old J. B.
Fighting fire in a clapboard shack
And stopping wind in an open crack.

Been everywhere a hat can go
In forty-eight states and Mexico
I've grown old as we trailed along
While you, old hat, are going strong.

You've been a good pal through all of that
You dirty, old gray, old Stetson hat.

STRAWBERRY ROAN

I was hangin' round town, just a-spendin' my time
Out of a job and not makin' a dime,
When a stranger steps up an' he says "I suppose
You are a bronc rider, by the looks of your clothes."

"You figures me right, an' I'm a good one, I claim.
Do you happen to have any bad ones to tame?"
He says he got one, an' a bad one to buck
An' at throwin' good riders, he's had lots of luck.

He says this ol' pony has never been rode,
An' all the boys that gets on him is bound to get throwed,
I gets up excited, an' asks what he pays.
If I'd ride this ol' pony a couple of days.

He offers a ten spot, an' I says "I'm your man!'
For the bronc never lived that I couldn't fan.
No the bronc never lived, nor never drew breath
That I couldn't ride til he starved plumb to death.

He says "get your saddle, an' I'll give you a chance."
So I gets in his buckboard and rides to his ranch.
I waits until mornin' an' right after chuck
I goes out to see if his outlaw can buck.

Down in the corral a'standin' alone
Was this ol' caballo, a strawberry roan.
He's ewe-necked an' old, with a long lower jaw,
I can see with one eye he's a reg'lar outlaw.

Little pin ears with a split at the tip,
An' a big 44 brand upon his left hip.
His legs were all spavined, and he's got pigeon toes,
Little pig eyes an' a big Roman nose.

I straps on my spurs, an' I'm sure feelin' fine
I pulls down my hat an' I coils up by twine.
I piles my loop on him and well, I knows then
That if he gets rode, I'll sure earn my ten.

I gets the blind on him, it sure is a fight.
Next comes the saddle, an' I screws 'er down tight.
I steps right up on him, an' raises the blind,
I'm right in his middle to see him unwind.

He bowed his ol' neck and I guess he unwound.
He seemed to quit livin' down there on the ground.
He went up towards the east an' came down towards the west,
An' to stay in his middle I sure done my best.

He turns his ol' belly right up to the sun,
He sure is a sun-fishin' sonnuvvagun.
An' when he's a-buckin' he squeals like a shoat,
I'll tell you this pony has sure got my goat.

I loses my stirrup, an' also my hat.
I start pullin' leather, I'm blind as a bat.
With a phenomenal jump he goes up, and on high,
Leaves me settin' on nothin' way up in the sky.

I turns over twice and comes down to the earth.
I starts in a-cussin' the day of his birth.
Now there might be some ponies that I cannot ride,
Some of 'em's livin', they haven't all died.

But I'll bet all my money that the man ain't alive,
Who can stay with ol' Strawberry, when he makes his high-dive!

THE STARS AND STRIPES

The Stars and Stripes, flag of the United States of America; the worldwide hope of all peoples who, under God, would be free to live and do His will. Upon its folds is written the story of America. The epic of the mightiest and noblest nation in all history.

In the days when peoples of the old world groveled in abject homage to the heresy of "The divine right of Kings", a new constellation appeared in the western skies. The Stars and Stripes, symbolizing the divine right of all men to life, liberty, happiness, and peace under endowment by their creator.

To what man is given words adequate enough to tell the story of the building of this nation? That immortal story is written in blood and sweat, in heroic deeds, and unremitting toil, in clearing of primeval forests and in burgeoning of the vast waters of prairies where the wild coyote and buffalo roamed and the red man claimed his solitary reign. Onward swept this empire of the western world, spanning wide rivers heedless of its onward march. Leaping vast mountain ranges leaving in its path villages and farms, factories and mines, till at last this giant nation stood astride the continent of the West. From Atlantic to Pacific, gasping in either hand horizons of the rising and setting sun.

This is the heritage of the people of these United States. It has been purchased by each succeeding generation and must be re-won by each succeeding generation until the end of time. The modern world in the vanity of its scientific and technological achievements may forget God; and when men forget their Creator their own creations will be turned upon them.

Only love, true love, of our fellow men can contain these world destroying implements. The emblem and token of that love is the Stars and Stripes, symbol of the American way of life, obedience under law.

We are proud of being called patriots. It labels us as loyal defenders of the Stars and Stripes, and the ideals of our country.

LETTERS FROM FRANCE

Henry Francis Deter was drafted into the Army in 1918, at the age of 24. He was sent to Camp Dix, New Jersey for basic training. After completing basic training, he was sent to France to serve in the First World War. We have only been able to find a few letters that he wrote home, the first from Camp Dix, and the rest from France. They are on very fragile paper and in poor condition. Following is a transcription of the letters, a few blanks have been inserted where words just could not be made out.

The envelopes are all addressed: Mrs. Julia Deter, Deer Trail, Colo. U.S. A. The return addresses are all the same as he has signed in each letter.

Some of the letters briefly mention the flu. At this time, the influenza epidemic was raging, and great numbers of people were dying from it all over the World (worse in the eastern United States and Europe). While at Camp Dix, one of Henry's duties was in the infirmary tending to men with influenza. The men who returned home after the war were very fortunate indeed to have survived not only World War I, but also the flu epidemic.

Camp Dix, NewJersey
Aug. 28, 18

Dear Ma,

Well we arrived here last night about twelve o'clock, after a long and tiresome trip. This is sure some camp, we have barracks here to live in. The streets are all hard as rock. We haven't had breakfast yet this morning, the cook had an awful time getting their outfit together after their trip. We came through some very interesting places coming up here. We were in eleven different states. We were in Pittsburgh, Pa. yesterday morning but couldn't see very much of the town. We stopped in Harrisburg the capital and had a parade about noon and last night we came through Philadelphia.

The Red Cross met us at the train and served ice cream and cigarettes nearly every place we stopped. They served something at Indianapolis, Ind. we had a big swim at a Y.M.C.A. building, the people are sure patriotic in this country.

We are only about twenty miles from the Atlantic Ocean here and about fifty miles from New York City.

Well I guess we will leave here soon for France from the way our officers talk. I haven't had a chance to see Fat[1] or Ole[2] yet but will hunt them up as soon as I get time, they got here a day or two ago.

We sure did come through some rough country coming up here. It is sure fine coming through Pa. and Ind. We never saw much of Ohio, we stopped once in Columbus, Ohio, but couldn't get off the train. They didn't allow anyone to get off without permission, but there were a couple of guys got lost nearly every time we had a parade, but they caught up with us before we got here. We were not supposed to throw off any mail along the road but we did. We were on the road from 8:30 Thursday morning to eleven last night.

Our train broke down in some little town in Missouri in the Ozark Mountains. We had some time there, we were there about two hours and they let us run around to suit ourselves. There were lots of people gathered around there in a little while. We sang all kinds of songs and they passed around cigars and candy. They said that was the biggest bunch of soldiers they had ever seen.

I am going to try and get a few days off and go see Aunt Tress[3] if I can, but we may not be here long. I heard we were to leave here in ten days, but we always hear a lot of stuff.

This is some camp, there is room here for 100,000 men here and it is all barracks.

When does Tom[4] and that bunch leave home, or does anyone know for sure.

Well I guess I will have to close and go to breakfast now. Hoping to hear from you soon.

From

Add. Pvt. Henry F. Deter
Co. E. 139 Inf.
Camp Dix
New Jersey

---

[1] We believe this to be – Floyd "Fat" Hanks, who married Henry's sister Josie in 1918.
[2] We believe this to be – Ole Smith, a friend and neighbor about Henry's age.
[3] Tress O'Connor, his Mother Julia's sister.
[4] May be Tom Price, one of Hank's buddies, about his age.

November 28, 1918

Dear Mother,

I suppose I had better write you a line or so to let you know that I am getting along fine and am well and this being Thanksgiving Day we are resting. We sure had a fine feast today. I will tell you about it, the first thing on the program was roast turkey, then dressing, potatoes, gravy, corn, bread and butter, and coffee, and there was plenty of it. I never ate supper and the way I feel now I won't need any breakfast. That isn't the only good meal we have had as nearly every day.

We are billeted in an old house in a little town called Corronibles. We have it pretty nice to. It is warm in most of these houses over here as they are built of stone about two feet thick, and the roofs are of tile. We have a fire place in ours and sometimes have a fire. These are funny towns or villages as they call them. The streets run in nearly every direction, and the houses are built every way imaginable. Sometimes there will be two or more families in the same house. There are no stores in this town so if we had any money we could not spend it here, but it isn't far to other towns close that a fellow can buy any thing you want lots of wine in particular.

It seems like most everything stays green here all winter, that is vegetables and stuff like that. The trees shed their leaves early in the fall. It has not frozen but a couple of times since we have been here. It rains a whole lot of the time and is muddy all of the time, anyway it has been every since we landed here. It was hard to get used to all of that mud, but I don't mind it at all now as we have drilled in it, slept in it, and it was a very common thing to see men that were all over mud as they were in the worst of it when they were in the trenches.

I guess I never did tell you about the trip we had across the ocean and England. Well we left New York on the 13th of October and put in ten days on the ocean. Never got a bit sick all the way, but some of the poor guys were sure enough sick. It was a very interesting trip and we had a little submarine scare one morning. Our torpedo boats fired several shots but they never shot any of the big guns.

Altogether we had sixteen ship loads of soldiers in the convoy. It was a pretty sight, early of a morning seemed to be the best time to get out on the deck and look around. Well we went around north of Ireland, then down between there and Scotland. We could see the east of both of the islands, finally we landed in Liverpool. We marched through quite a bit of the town, it is some place.

We were marched into a big railroad and got onto a train. It had places in it for eight men in a place, and there were five of these little compartments to a coach. We traveled from there to Camp Codford at Codford, England. We rested up there for about four days and left for South Hampden, England where we got on a boat and crossed the English Channel to LeHavre, France. It took us all night, we had to lay in the harbor all day and wait the tide to come up. After we got off, we marched through the town up on a big hill into an old army camp.

They put thirteen of us in a tent and believe me it was sure crowded. We stayed there a couple of days and marched back to the station. They loaded us onto what is called side door Pullman cars, in other words they are boxcars. Well they put thirty of us in a car. We thought that was awful, but we had to ride for two days and nights.

We finally got to Le Mans, we were marched out to a camp and put up our tents, which we did in about an hour we got orders to move. Well we marched about five miles and were lined up in a place and told we were to stay there all night. The mud was at least four inches deep and it was raining. Well we got some straw and made our beds down there. Although it was that muddy I slept about as good as I ever did in my life. The next morning we got orders to move again, and were marched out to the camp we came from the night before. There we stayed in the rain and mud for three days. We then got out of there and got on a train. We didn't know where we were going but we rode for two days and nights, it was pretty cold in those boxcars, and it rained all of the time.

We finally got off at a little town close to the front lines called LesIslittes. We put our tents up and stayed there about an hour, then we moved again. We went to a small town the Germans had torn all to pieces with their big guns. There we were transferred to the outfit we are with now. We stayed there two days and it looked like we were going to the trenches, but one morning the message came down that the Huns had signed the Armistice. You can't imagine how glad the bunch were as the new bunch we were with then had just came from the front lines, and they had told us about getting all shot up.

We finally left there and went to another camp and we had good barracks there. We stayed there about a week and moved again, and here we are.

Well don't worry about me as I am in the best of health and will get along fine, and as the war is practically over, we will come back to America, which we hope will be very soon.

Hoping this finds you all well and wishing you a Merry Christmas and a happy New Year.

       From
        Henry,
Add. Henry F. Deter
Co K 309 Inf.
A.E.F.

Somewhere in France
Dec 25, 1918

Dear Mother,

I will try and drop you a few lines to let you know that I am getting along alright. I have had a bad cold for a short time but am alright.

We are having rain over here all the time and it snowed a few days ago only about two inches is about all and it went off in a little while. It never gets very cold here but it is sloppy under foot all the time but we _____ all of the time.

We had a fine dinner Xmas but it was nothing like being at home, we got a nice little package from the Y.M.C.A. with candy, tobacco and cigarettes in it.

It is hard telling when we will be home, some think we are to stay here and do guard duty in Germany for a year or so and some think we will be back sometime before spring. Well we are all hoping to leave here soon most of the boys are getting pretty tired of this country.

We have been here a little over two months now and I have never gotten a letter from anyone yet but hope to soon.

I suppose it is awful cold there now. I saw a New York paper and I see they are having snow there and blizzards. Have any of the boys from Deer Trail come home since the Armistice was signed. I guess most of them are over here somewhere but I have never seen one of them. I have heard the outfit Fat and Ole were with were in one of the last strikes the Americans made and I am anxious to know whether they both came out alright. I guess I was a pretty lucky guy we just got over here and joined this outfit a day or two before the peace was signed.

Well guess I will have to close for this time. Hoping this finds you all well and happy and wishing you a Happy New Year,

I remain
Henry
Pvt. Henry F. Deter
Co. K. 309 Inf. 78 Division
A.E.F.

Bard – France
Jan. 17, 1919

Dear Mother,

I rec'd your first letter day before yesterday and you can't imagine how glad I was to hear from you, that was my first letter from the states since I sailed from N. Y. I was a little home sick for a little while got over it in a short time though. One of your letters was dated Dec. 22nd and one from the 24th. I also got the card Joe sent me on the 22nd of Dec. was glad I got the addresses of Fat and Ole. I am looking every day for those good things you sent me and all of the back letters. I know I must have a lot of them.

Well I was surprised to hear that Tom had gone to training camp. But he is sure lucky to be on that side of the big pond. He won't have to stay in the service very long, and the guys on this side can't tell for sure just when they will be back and there are a lot of them that will never come back. Good old Grant Smith, I was sure sorry to hear that he got picked off and just a day or so before the Armistice was signed. Well every time I think of it I feel that I am one of the most fortunate guys in the world.

They must be having an awful hard winter at home this year from the way your letter reads and from what the papers say. Well I don't know whether it is bad here or not it only rains all of the time. I would rather have the snow any old time. The mud is a couple of inches deep everywhere but on the roads and they are about as hard as rock, that is about the only thing they have over here that amounts to anything. Well the horses are some of the best I ever saw but they don't have very many of them.

What was the matter with Harlow? He is sure having an awful time, if very many more things happen to him he will sure enough ____.

Well Ma I will close for this time this leaves me fine and dandy and I hope it will find you the same. Hoping to hear from you soon.

remain,

Henry F. Deter
Co. K. 309 Inf. 78 Div.
A.E.F.

Dear Mother,

Rec'd your letter yesterday, the one dated Feb. 3rd. It made pretty good time getting over here about eighteen days. It is very funny that I haven't rec'd any more than that. We have very poor mail service over here, and if that xmas box was of any great value you had better get some of those Red Cross workers to try and trace it _____. I don't see any reason why they wouldn't be able to find it nearly all of the boys that were transferred to this outfit the same time that I was got all of their back mail and I can't understand why I never got mine.

I'm still feeling fine but will have to be very careful as the Flu is raging around here again. It surely is a bad thing, I saw my share of it while we were camped at Camp Dix and I hope it don't get bad again. That is too bad about Ad Ernst but it can't be helped. I am afraid if they don't take the boys home pretty soon there is going to be a lot of them left buried over here. The people in the east are raising an awful fuss now about the boys over here. They are not being taken care of the way they expect and I don't think it any more than right after buying all of those liberty bonds they ought to have something to say.

I got one of your letters with some clippings from the papers but I have never rec'd any mail from Aunt Tress yet. I can't understand about the box you speak of sent to me from a Paris, France store, who in the world would be sending me a box from there.

I have written Ole and Pat from here. I think Jane sent me their adds. some time ago but they have never answered as yet, I am going to try again. I also wrote Lillian[5] a letter but she must have forgotten that such a human as me ever existed.

Did all of the boys that you mentioned in your letter as returning get a discharge or are they just home on a furlough. Well I don't blame Tom for wanting to get home but he ought to be over here it would sure enough try his patience.

It seems very strange that Aunt Carrie[6] would come to visit me at Camp Dix and never let me know anything about it. I could possibly have gone to see them although they could not get in on account of the quarantine. I am going to try and visit some of those folks if I am mustered out in Camp Dix.

Wish I could be there to take in some of those dances. We have had a couple of French dances here in this town since I have been here it is lots of fun to watch them hop around, some of the American boys try it but with very little success.

---

[5] We believe this is Lillian Ross, evidently a girlfriend of Henry's before the war.

[6] Carrie O'Connor, another of Henry's Mother Julia's sisters.

What has become of Aunt Alice you never say anything about her. I don't know whether she knows I am over here or not maybe it don't make any difference anyway.

I am sending you a clipping from a news paper this is a very old country right here where we are camped and you can get part of the history out of this little story most of the places that are mentioned are very near here. You can look at any big map of France and find Semus it is about six miles from here. I am also enclosing some post cards of some old places we were to visit yesterday.

Well I will have to close hoping this finds you all well.

From
Pvt. Henry F. Deter
Co. K. 309 Inf. 78 Division
R. E. F.

The following is the last page of a letter. It was found alone in an envelope dated Feb. 1919. I included it because, although it does not say much without the rest of the letter, it does speak of him making plans, while in France, about his return home, and hoping there would still be land left for him by the time he got home.

(I hope)[7] to get one of those homesteads that the U. S. are going to offer to the boys. There are sure going to be a lot of them come west and take land, and it won't take very long before it will be all gone.

Well guess I will have to close for this time. Hoping to hear from you soon, and that this finds you all well.

Good by,

Pvt. Henry F. Deter
Co. K 309 Inf. 78 Division
A. P. O. 755
France

---

[7] implied

CHINKING MIXTURE

This is not a story, but was found amongst his writings. It is a recipe for making chinking. Chinking was used to fill and seal the cracks between logs in a log building. It's not in great demand in this day and age, and probably will never be again. How many people are left in this world that know the secret of a good chinking mixture. It's a piece of history soon to fade away.

2 parts clay (or dirt)

1 part sifted wood ashes

½ part salt

(Hydrated lime can be used as a substitute for the ashes)

Mix each batch slowly. It will take some experimenting to get the right consistency.

The following is a letter, written by my Grandfather, Henry Deter, to the Union Pacific Railroad, on behalf of the Deer Trail Pioneer Historical Society, in 1968. The letter evidently did not have the desired effect, toward the cause they were fighting for, as the Union Pacific Depot in Deer Trail, was indeed closed in 1969.

This letter will be signed by the officers of the Deer Trail Pioneer Historical Society, who are descendants of pioneer settlers in this part of Colorado. All of these and many more of our people helped to make the Union Pacific a great Railroad.

1969 will be the 100th anniversary of the railway coming through Deer Trail. Also the 100th anniversary of the first celebration, where was held the first Bronco Busting contest, and other cowboy events, ever held anywhere. Our society is making plans for a pageant to commemorate this anniversary.

Our Colorado history tells us that Deer Trail was the largest shipping point in Colorado Territory at one time. Many thousands of cattle and sheep and horses, many carloads of wool and wheat have been shipped from Deer Trail. We realize the freight and passenger business is gone, since the march of progress has brought us the super highway, the autos and trucks, and airlines.

We are appealing to the Railroad and Colorado P.U.C. to reconsider and change their plans, and handle all of their freight traffic through the agency at Deer Trail. This change would not create any additional expense to the railroad and would add much to the historical and colorful past of Deer Trail.

We especially condemn and regret the closing of the depot at Deer Trail.

Following are two articles out of the Rocky Mt. News, which Henry had copied down. The first dated June 15, 1875, the second, June 18, 1875. They are about a "Roundup" held at the Wilson Ranch near Godfrey, Colorado.

Following that is an article, written by Henry in 1975, evidently to advertise a "Roundup" re-creation and Chuck wagon dinner put on by the Deer Trail Pioneer Historical Society to celebrate the 100th anniversary of this event.

Rocky Mountain News, June 15, 1875

A Cattle Roundup

A roundup of cattle will be held at the Wilson's ranch, about twelve miles from Godfrey[1] station, on the Kansas Pacific, in Elbert County, on Wednesday and Thursday. Parties who may be curious to witness this remarkable phase of outdoor life on the plains, can do so by taking the Kansas Pacific train tomorrow morning, returning to the city on Thursday. Teams will convey the excursionists from Godfrey to the ranch and back. It will be necessary for those who go to provide themselves with blankets. The Wilson brothers will furnish the excursionists with meals, and transport them from the station to the ranch free of charge. Tickets for the round trip $6.00. The train will leave Denver at 7:45 a.m.

Rocky Mountain News, June 18, 1875

A Roundup on the Plains

The grand "Roundup" of cattle at Wilson's ranch, twelve miles from Godfrey, on Wednesday and Thursday, was witnessed by two or three hundred people, including a delegation of Denverites. Everybody seemed pleased with the hospitality so freely and generously extended by the Wilson Brothers.

A large number of Indians were present. Wednesday night a moonlight dance was indulged in until about two o'clock yesterday morning. The number of cattle collected in all that region of the country since the roundup season commenced is about 100,000 head.

---

[1] Godfrey station was six miles south of Agate, Colorado. The name was later changed to Buick.

This year's celebration will surpass anything we have ever attempted in portraying a century of progress in this great country. A thousand details, the work of many individuals scores of exhibits and displays and a full quota of events will be coordinated into an outstanding program to be presented.

What – A celebration of the good old West. A reunion of men and women who have made and are making Gods country and its traditions. They are going to come from all over Colorado to help share in this 100th anniversary of the big roundup.

Where – At Deer Trail, Colorado, where lingers the romance of the Old West, where the climate's cool and the handshake is warm.

When – Mid-summer, June 7, 1975. When its vacation time. When it's cool in Colorado. When it's the 100th home coming for cowboys and cowgirls.

Why – Because it's the romance of the Old West and we love it. Because the first roundups were held near Deer Trail. Because we want to promote fellowship between the people of the area in this "second century". Because we want to have Deer Trail recognized as an historical shrine to the "Spirit of the Old West". Because we invite you to make camp with us so you can love it too.

How – Saddle up the old gas buggy and roll in. The roads are good and we like folks.

It's our 7th Annual Chuck Wagon Dinner
Saturday, June 7, 1975 at Centennial Park in Deer Trail

BEST EXHIBITS:
Booths filled with nearly anything you could want to see, with prettier gals as booth attendants than our exhibitors have had in the previous shows.

BEST PROGRAM:
This year's program, with emphasis on the many steps you can be taking and the planning in these uncertain times, has something for everyone, and includes demonstrations you really should plan to see. The whole program is really great, don't miss it.

BEST PARTIES:
The theme is Western and we will dedicate Centennial Park. Parties have been increased in size this year. With entertainment that is different and with all the food you can consume in the evening.

We will commemorate the roundup at Wilson's ranch, June 15, 1875. A highlight of the day will be the dedication of our Centennial Community Flag. We will present other skits and exhibition dancing of our forefathers.

BEST CROWDS:
We will bet you will find friends you have not seen in years! Before you finish reading this make plans to attend this grand "Roundup", a thrilling and interesting picturazation. Be here for the celebration depicting some of the Pioneer Past and the Progressive Present. Visualize a great cattle roundup with cowboys and cowgirls, cattlemen, and cow horses, and chuck wagons.

EPILOGUE

The stories in this book pretty much cover my Grandfather's life as an early day pioneer and cowboy. They are probably pretty typical of a lot of the early day cowboys and pioneers. I would like to conclude with a little about the rest of his life, as I know it.

He spent the first 32 years of his life as an old west cowboy. Most of the time on a horse, as not only his work but also his recreation took place on the back of a horse. After the turn of the century, things began slowly changing as the west became more settled. By the time Henry returned home from World War One in 1919 the country was covered with homesteaders and barb wire fences. There were no more roundups and fewer jobs for cowboys on the remaining smaller ranches in the area. So he began trying to make a little money with a few head of cattle of his own.

Then he married my Grandmother, Helen Compton, in 1926, at the age of 32, and began raising a family. A few years later, the depression and dust bowl hit. Grandpa always said he couldn't tell that the depression made much difference to them, as they were really poor and struggling before it hit. But the drought of the dust bowl years had an impact, especially when you were barely eking out a living farming and ranching. Everyone of that era tells the stories of the clouds of dust moving across the country so thick that you couldn't see out the windows. Hanging damp sheets over the windows in an attempt to keep some of it out of the house so you could breathe. Setting the table with the plates upside down to keep them clean until the meal was put on the table.

He worked at various jobs in the area, including purchasing pinto beans for the Peoria Elevator, and hauling milk for the Colorado Milk Producers to Deer Trail where it was loaded on a train and shipped to Denver. In 1935 they purchased a ranch east of Deer Trail where they raised sheep, cattle, wheat, and beans over the years, and eventually expanded the ranch to over three thousand acres. My Mother says she remembers Grandpa always working hard, because everything you did in those days was hard work.

Henry developed asthma in later years and because of it retired early from ranching, leasing the land out to his daughter and son-in-law. He purchased a liquor store in Deer Trail, which he and Helen operated for a time. They sold it and bought an old vacant building that had been the lumber company in Deer Trail, and remodeled it into the "Rocket" restaurant. It was so named because of the missile base, which was being built just north of town at that time. The restaurant did a very good business because of the missile base workers. After only a few years he sold this to the BPOE for an Elks lodge.

He was always active in the community. He was a charter member of the Deer Trail Jockey Club, secretary of the School Board for fourteen years, served on the Soil Conservation Board, charter member of the Elks Lodge, and an active member of the American Legion Post.

His love and knowledge of local history and its preservation led to his helping organize the Deer Trail Pioneer Historical Society in 1969. That became a passion for him, from then on he spent a lot of time working to establish and maintain the museum in the old Deer Trail Depot building. He found an old chuckwagon, fixed it up, and used it to serve "Chuckwagon Dinners" to raise money for the Historical Society. He, with the aide of other dedicated Historical Society Members, would cook steak and biscuits in dutch ovens, beans and coffee in a huge pots over an open fire, like his Dad cooked for the cattle drives years ago. They were very successful and would draw large crowds from all over eastern Colorado.

In 1980, Henry and Helen sold the ranch and moved to Deer Trail. He always stayed busy, loved to tinker and repair old things. He collected arrowheads and rocks. He even polished rocks and made some fine jewelry for a while until the dust got to his asthma. He loved to play cards and would rustle up a game at about every family gathering of more than two or three people. He would also play a little pitch with the boys in town and at the local Turkey Shoots. He loved children and couldn't resist giving them a little teasing once in a while. He had an old black poodle-cross dog named Jack that was his companion after he retired. They spent lots of hours riding around in the pick-up together, looking over the ranch.

I was always struck by how well educated he seemed, and was, for only an eighth grade, one room school house education. This can be seen in these stories he wrote, and boy, you didn't want to try to beat him at Trivial Pursuit! He also liked to talk about the history of the area, and would tell lots of stories and facts besides the ones written here. Because none of us are ever good at writing down or remembering those oral accounts, most of them have been lost.

Henry Frances Deter passed away, April 28, 1986 at the age of 91, he is buried in the Evergreen Cemetery in Deer Trail. He remained active until a few months before his death.

About the Author

Henry Frances Deter 1894-1986

Henry f. Deter spent his lifetime writing, but not professionally. This is the first publication of his complete writings, almost twenty years after his death. He contributed to some small booklets published by the Deer Trail Pioneer Historical Society. Many friends and family members have enjoyed his stories over the years, but he, as most people, never considered events of his lifetime as history. A lot of his writing was done after he retired, probably between the ages of 70 and 90.

Henry was a member of that amazing generation that saw so many significant changes in their lifetime. Things we take for granted today, such as a telephone, an automobile, and a refrigerator, were all phenomenal inventions within his lifetime.

Printed in the United States
42012LVS00007B/256-306